CONTROL YOUR DEPRESSION

CONTROL YOUR DEPRESSION

Revised and Updated

Peter M. Lewinsohn, Ph.D.
Ricardo F. Muñoz, Ph.D.
Mary Ann Youngren, Ph.D.
Antonette M. Zeiss, Ph.D.

PRENTICE
HALL
PRESS

New York   London   Toronto   Sydney   Tokyo

Prentice Hall Press
15 Columbus Circle
New York, New York 10023

PRENTICE HALL PRESS and colophon are registered
trademarks of Simon & Schuster Inc.

Library of Congress Cataloging-in-Publication Data
Main Entry Under Title:
Control your depression.
   1. Depression, Mental.   2. Self-care, Health.
I. Lewinsohn, Peter M.
RC537.C68   1986   616.85'27   85-25570
ISBN 0-13-171893-2

Printed in the United States of America

10   9   8   7   6

To the many clients and colleagues
who—over the years—have
helped us develop this approach
to treating depression

Contents

Preface

Since the publication of the original edition, considerable progress has been made in our understanding of depression. There is increasing recognition by the mental health professions and by the general public that depression is even more common than previously thought. Recent scientific studies indicate that between 10% and 20% of the general adult population has been depressed at some time in their lives. In some community studies, as many as 50% of participants have a history of depression. Appropriately, depression has been called "the common cold of mental health." These statistics have at least two implications: a) There are many people who need help to assist them with overcoming their depression; and b) depression is not some kind of rare disease. Rather, serious depression is a relatively common problem, and feelings of depression are a universal part of human experience.

It is also becoming increasingly clear that depression occurs through the entire age span. We now know that occasionally young children become depressed, that depression is fairly common in adolescents, and that depression is the most frequent mental health problem for older people. Although we have more objective information about depression in adults than in children and adolescents, there is agreement among experts that even in these young people depression is a growing problem.

The presence of depression is often more difficult to recognize in elderly individuals. Many of the symptoms of depression, like feelings of sadness, lethargy and fatigue, difficulties with thinking and memory, and loss of interest in social activities, are often *erroneously* attributed to "normal aging." We now know that older persons who are physically healthy show relatively little decline in their mental and emotional functioning. Older persons who feel pessimistic, tired, and unmotivated and who are worried about their memory and concentration may very well be depressed.

Depression is an important clinical problem not only because of the suffering and distress that are associated with being depressed, but also because being depressed has serious negative effects on one's ability to function in everyday life. Depression has been shown to interfere with one's ability to think and concentrate, with one's social behavior and motivation. Being depressed thus seriously reduces one's ability to function adaptively and to cope with the normal problems of daily life. It is therefore especially important to overcome depression as quickly as possible. This book is intended to help you achieve this goal.

We have also learned that most people who become depressed do not seek professional help and that people differ in how long it takes them to overcome their depression. Some are able to do so in a few weeks or months. Others may take a year or more. The methods found in this book are intended to shorten the duration of an episode of depression.

Although this book is written primarily for people who are depressed, it may also be useful for people who are not depressed now, but who have been depressed in the past. Similarly, people who have not had problems with depression in the past, but who are about to enter new situations which may be stressful, may want to become familiar with the techniques described in this book to reduce the likelihood of becoming seriously depressed as a result of the upcoming life changes.

As we recognized in the earlier edition, a substantial number of people need some help and encouragement to make use of a self-help book such as this one. It is for this reason that we have developed a "Coping with Depression Course" in which people meet as a group to work on each of the chapters together. These courses, which are conducted like a small seminar, have typically held twelve meetings over a period of eight weeks with five to ten participants. Each meeting focuses on a specific chapter of *Control Your Depression*. An instructor's manual, *The Coping with Depression Course* (Castella Press., 1984), is available for the leaders of these groups.*

Many of the techniques described in this book have been used in more than 50 scientifically controlled treatment outcome studies in which they have shown to be efficacious, sometimes singly, but most often in combination.

Coping with Depression courses, for which *Control Your Depression* has served as the textbook, have been evaluated in five scientific studies. In all of these studies, the experience has been associated with improvement in approximately 80% of the participants. The courses have been used at the University of Oregon, Arizona State University, the Palo Alto Veterans Administration Hospital, and Portland State University.

*The Instructor's Manual is available from Castalia Publishing Co., PO Box 1587, Eugene, OR 97440.

Work presently being conducted by the Depression Prevention Research Project of the University of California, San Francisco, is examining whether people who learn the techniques described in this book are less likely to become seriously depressed in the future. This work is being done with medical patients, who have been found to be a higher risk for depression than non-medical populations. As this edition of our book goes to press, this research project is just beginning. Thus, final results are not available. The logic of the study is as follows: if people who are already depressed can benefit from learning and using these techniques, perhaps the use of the techniques can help prevent people from becoming depressed in the first place.

Feelings of depression are part of human experience, of course, and we do not expect to prevent feelings of depression altogether. We *do* intend to reduce 1) the frequency of serious episodes of depression, 2) the duration of any such episode, and 3) the severity or intensity of depression during any one episode.

CONTROL YOUR DEPRESSION

Introduction

Alice has been feeling low for about eight months now. Like everyone else, she has had "down" periods before, but they have usually not lasted this long. She doesn't feel like doing much, has had trouble sleeping and eating, has lost her sense of humor, and is starting to wonder whether she is ever going to feel better.

Her relationship with her family has her worried. She feels that she is a burden on them and that her gloominess is affecting her husband and teenage children. Her job responsibilities are also a source of concern. As a real estate agent, she finds that her pace is generally quite fast. But in the past few months, she has slowed down considerably. She is just not functioning as efficiently as she used to. And though she has tried, she can't get herself motivated.

Alice is tired of feeling sad and blue. But even worse, she is afraid that there may be something seriously wrong with her. At times she's even wondered whether she might be losing control, having a "mental breakdown," or even going crazy. She just doesn't understand what is happening to her and doesn't know how to overcome her distress. Yet her doctor tells her that there is nothing physically wrong with her.

Alice is experiencing depression, one of the most common of psychological problems. Mild feelings of depression are experienced by almost everyone at some time. In some cases feelings of depression become so intense and last so long that professional help becomes advisable.

Psychologists and psychiatrists have not yet discovered all they would like to know about depression. There are many ideas about what produces it and what keeps it going, and there are a number of treatments designed to deal with it.

This book is intended to explain one approach and to give specific steps that are useful in controlling depression. The ideas and techniques presented here are the ones we use in working with people who seek help because they feel seriously depressed, as well as in classes designed to prevent depression in people who are well.

1

How This Book Is Organized

This book is divided into three parts: Part I tells you how we think about depression. Chapter 1 explains what psychologists mean by *depression* and how to recognize it. Chapter 2 describes the psychological framework we use in making sense out of human behavior—that is, how we explain why people behave the way they do. It is known as the *social learning approach*. Chapter 3 brings together depression and social learning and explains how to use this approach to deal with depression.

Part II presents strategies for controlling depression. We describe step-by-step procedures so that you can use these methods on your own. Chapter 4 helps you to decide which method to try first, and Chapters 5 through 11 give detailed instructions on the techniques we have found useful. Here is where you will learn specific ways to control depression.

Part III is about ensuring success. It concerns using the ideas you have learned to deal with future circumstances. Chapter 12 explains ways to maintain your gains and to help prevent the return of serious depression. Chapter 13 describes ways to extend the skills you have learned to other areas of your life. Chapter 14 explores the idea of planning your future and the psychological advantages of having clarified your goals and purposes in life.

Some Characteristics of This Book

We have attempted to be as concrete as possible in our explanation and instructions, avoiding useless generalities. We have included ways to check whether you are using the techniques properly and how much progress you are making. It is important that you *individualize* what we suggest. Not every technique will be useful to all readers; we have included a variety so that you can find those techniques that will work for you.

Because the book is really intended to teach a way of *thinking* about depression as well as controlling it, you may find it useful even if depression is not a problem for you at present. For example, it can give you ideas for preventing depression. Teachers may find the techniques easy to share with their students. Finally, the social learning approach can be helpful as a way of thinking about how you behave in many other situations and how to change behavior that is problematic.

Improving Your Chances for Success

How can you increase the likelihood that using this book will help *you* to overcome your depression? Although we do not have precise answers to this difficult question, we do have some ideas and suggestions based on our experiences with people who have used the book and benefitted from the experience:

1. Read the book *and* do the exercises in a systematic way. Just reading the book is not enough. The exercises should be done for the recommended period of time. It has been our experience that people who actually do the exercises are the ones who benefit the most.

2. Pay attention to your attitude. Depression is accompanied by feelings of helplessness and hopelessness, which contribute to the attitude that you have very little control over your life and future. This attitude is not conducive to undertaking the task of reading the chapters and doing the exercises. It is important, therefore, for you to remind yourself that there *is* the possibility that you *will* gain greater control over yourself and your emotions as you follow our suggestions. This reminder is necessary to motivate you to try the techniques. As they begin to work, your conviction that change *is* possible will grow. We have found that people who can learn to think that they have some control over their life, that what their life is going to be five years from now can be influenced by what they do now, and that they are not completely at the mercy of external forces are more likely to have long-term success with these methods.

A second attitude that is helpful is considering your periods of nondepressed mood your normal state of being. That is, periods in which you are depressed do not reflect "the real you." When you are depressed you generally feel pessimistic, which leads you to believe that you are always going to experience the symptoms of depression, such as poor sleep, poor appetite, lethargy, lack of interest and pleasure in things that you used to enjoy. Instead of letting these expectations occupy your mind, think back to periods when you did not feel depressed, when you were energetic, involved, and interested. Try to remind yourself that such a healthy state is your normal way of being, "the real you." You will go back to feeling this way once the depression is over. By keeping this objective in mind, you will be able to use the ideas in the book more effectively, because they will become the tools which will get you back to your usual state of mind.

A third attitude that is helpful is that it is OK to enlist the help and support of someone else. This could be a family member, a friend, a minister, anybody you trust. The idea is to find someone who is interested enough in you so that they are willing to discuss the chapters with you, review the exercises with you, and provide you with other assistance as it may be needed. Although it is possible to benefit from this book by yourself, you can increase the likelihood of success by setting up a "buddy system" with someone who can do a little bit of pacing, reinforcing, offering encouragement, and so on.

The final attitude that we would like to discuss is skepticism. People who feel that reading the book and doing the exercises are important activities, and who consider the time devoted to getting better a serious investment in their wellbeing, are most likely to benefit. People who maintain a skeptical, cynical attitude as they go through the book are least likely to improve. Skepticism can be a helpful attitude at times. But when one is depressed, it can serve as a stumbling block. Skepticism calls into question the advice you get from others (including books like this one), and keeps you from giving them a good try. It becomes the source of a self-fulfilling prophecy: You question whether these ideas will work, so you don't use the ideas properly, and thus they do not work. You then feel vindicated (you were right, they don't work), but still depressed. It may be more practical to give these ideas the benefit of the doubt, give them an adequate try, and, once you are feeling better, subject them to whatever skeptical analysis you would like.

Feelings of depression are influenced by a large variety of factors. This book shows you how to use these factors to increase your control over depression. In this section, we have suggested ways to improve the chances that the book will be helpful to you. We hope that you will use these suggestions and that as you use the methods in the book, you will find that you can indeed control your depression.

A Word of Caution

This book is primarily intended to help people control their own depression. However, as noted in the preface, people often fail to complete self-help programs because it's difficult to maintain sufficient motivation when working alone on problems. Therefore, we encourage you to select a therapist, a counselor, or some other resource person to read this book, check on your progress from time to time, offer encouragement, and lend a helping hand if you get bogged down.

Furthermore, there is at least one situation in which we feel that you should seek help from a professional *immediately*, and that is when you are afraid you might commit suicide. During serious cases of depression, some people give up hope and may do things that they would not consider doing when they no longer feel depressed.

Not every difficult life situation is a result of depression or is likely to lead to it. There are other psychological problems that cause distress. These might include relationship problems, difficult decisions, fears of certain objects or situations, economic hardship, physical illness, and so on. You should seriously consider whether you are using this book as a way of avoiding dealing with a serious life situation that requires professional help. Any book, no matter how well written, has its limitations. If you have serious doubts that depression is your major problem, you might profit from a consultation with a mental health professional. To contact a professional helper, consult your local community mental health center, the Mental Health Association, your physician, or a member of the clergy. In most areas, licensed or certified psychologists, psychiatrists, and social workers are listed in the classified section of the telephone directory.

A Final Note

If you are sure that your problem is depression and have tried conscientiously to use the techniques we suggest but have found no relief, please do not conclude that your case is hopeless. What you have learned is that *this* method did not work for you. There are other methods. You should consider seeing a professional.

part one
THE CONCEPTS

1

Depression

Everyone has times of feeling sad or blue. People often refer to these feelings by saying they are "depressed." In this book we are discussing depression that differs in three ways from the "down" or "blue" periods that nearly everyone experiences:

1. The depression is more intense.
2. The depression lasts longer.
3. The depression significantly interferes with effective day-to-day functioning.

By "depression" we do *not* mean an ailment that a person *has*, like a disease or a broken leg. Rather, we see depression as something a person experiences or feels for a period of time. Sometimes the beginning of a period of depression is clear and dramatic and is related to a specific event, such as the death of a loved one. Grief and sorrow in these instances are natural reactions to personal loss. However, if the period of depression seems unduly prolonged, then it is time to do something about it. More often, though, there is no easily identifiable event that precedes depression. Rather, depression is experienced from time to time without any obvious explanation.

What Depression Is Not

First, being depressed is *not* abnormal or crazy. In fact, it is one of the most common problems people experience. According to recent studies, between 10 percent and 20 percent of adults in the United States will experience an episode of depression serious enough that professional help is advisable.

Second, depression is not just *any* bad or upsetting feeling. For example, depression is not feeling anxious or nervous, although it is true that depressed individuals frequently feel anxious as well as depressed. The point is that depression is not the only way of being distressed. This book is intended for persons who are depressed.

This chapter is devoted to a discussion of the specific set of behaviors and feelings that make up what we call *the depressive syndrome*. We have also included a questionnaire to help you decide if you are experiencing the kind of depression that can be helped by reading and using this book.

The Depressive Syndrome

A *syndrome* is a collection of events, behaviors, or feelings that often— *but not always*—go together. The depressive syndrome is a collection of rather specific feelings and behaviors that have been found to be characteristic of depressed persons *as a group*. It is important to recognize that there are large individual differences as to which of these feelings or behaviors are experienced and to what extent they are experienced. The following paragraphs discuss characteristics of the depressive syndrome.

DYSPHORIA

By *dysphoria*, we mean an unpleasant feeling state or—more simply— feeling bad. Dysphoria is the opposite of euphoria (feeling very happy) and is probably the most common symptom of depression. People who are depressed usually say they are feeling very sad, blue, hopeless, or "down" much of the time. They may see life as meaningless and are likely to be gloomy or pessimistic about the future. People vary in how they express these bad feelings. Some people look unhappy much of the time and cry very easily and more frequently than usual. Others manage to put up a good front much of the time, but inside they feel just as sad and dejected.

LOW LEVEL OF ACTIVITY

People are considerably less active when they are depressed than when they are not depressed. Sometimes a depressed person's typical day consists largely of sitting around and doing nothing or engaging in mostly passive, solitary activities like watching television, eating, or napping.

Going to work or taking care of daily household chores may seem to require an almost overwhelming amount of effort.

Often the depressed person feels unmotivated to engage in hobbies or other activities that formerly were enjoyable or satisfying. Such activities no longer appeal to the person and seem like just another chore that would require too much effort.

PROBLEMS INTERACTING WITH OTHER PEOPLE

Many depressed people express concern about their personal relationships. This concern may be expressed in a variety of ways. Some individuals are very unhappy and dissatisfied with their family relationships (with their spouses, parents, or children) or with other close, ongoing relationships. Some feel very uncomfortable, shy, and anxious when they are with other people, especially in a group. Others have difficulty coping with certain kinds of interactions, especially those in which they would like to be more assertive (for example, saying "no" to unreasonable demands or being more open and honest about their feelings). Finally, some depressed people feel lonely or unloved, but at the same time they are unwilling or unable to reach out to others even when they have opportunities for doing so.

FEELINGS OF WORTHLESSNESS AND INADEQUACY

Depressed people frequently describe themselves as failures, particularly in regard to areas that are of special personal importance to them (for example, family life, intellectual pursuits, or job performance). Sometimes these feelings of inadequacy appear unjustified to other people. For example, a woman may be considered very competent by her co-workers, but because her work falls short of her own standards of perfection, she puts herself down and feels like a total failure. Or a man who has recently lost his job may still be respected by his family and friends but nevertheless feels unworthy because he is no longer the breadwinner for his family.

GUILT

Some depressed persons express feelings of guilt and believe that they deserve to be punished for their "badness" or "sinfulness." Others feel guilt because of their failure—real or imagined—to assume responsibilities in their family lives or jobs. Such persons often feel they are a burden to others and blame themselves for being depressed and thereby failing to meet the needs of their families or others.

FEELING BURDENED

Some individuals do not feel any responsibility for their own depression; instead, they blame their distress on external causes. Such persons typically complain that other people frequently put excessive demands upon them. For example, a woman may feel constantly burdened by the demands her husband and children place upon her; she may believe that she would stop feeling depressed if these demands suddenly vanished.

PROBLEMS CONCENTRATING

Depressed people commonly experience trouble concentrating while they work on a problem or read a book or article or even as they try to follow a plot of a TV movie. They report that their thinking seems slowed down or that they feel somehow not as efficient and as clear in their problem-solving ability as they used to be. Sometimes this kind of problem will be especially noticeable when they must make decisions. The depressed person will find that making decisions that used to be simple (for example, what to buy for dinner or how to plan the day's activities) becomes difficult and troublesome.

PHYSICAL PROBLEMS

A common problem among depressed people is having a low level of energy with no obvious explanation. Depressed people frequently complain of feeling lethargic and fatigued, not just for a day or two but over an extended period.

Sleep disturbances of some kind are also common. Depressed people often have trouble falling asleep at night, or they sleep very restlessly with periods of wakefulness during the night. Others awaken very early—earlier than they need to arise—and are not able to return to sleep. Still others seem to sleep excessively—that is, they seem to require much more sleep than they used to.

Depressed people sometimes experience a loss of appetite and report that they no longer enjoy their food or eat irregularly; such people often show a weight loss even though they aren't trying to lose weight. On the other hand, some depressed people find that they eat more, especially between meals, when they are depressed and end up gaining weight even though they don't want to.

Other physical problems associated with depression include increased frequency and severity of headaches, stomachaches, and intestinal difficulties. Also, some depressed persons report reduced interest in sexual activity.

Again, it is important to remember that these features of the depressive syndrome are characteristic of depressed persons *as a group;* the depressed individual typically experiences only *some* of them. For example, a person's feelings may be dominated by sadness and hopelessness without his experiencing any guilt. Or someone may feel "slowed down" and fatigued without having headaches.

Another important point is that many characteristics of the depressive syndrome are commonly associated with various physical diseases. A person who has the flu, for example, is likely to have a low energy level, will not want to be around people, and generally feels "down." If you are experiencing some of the problems described and have not had a physical examination for a long time or have reason to question your physical health, we urge you to see your physican.

Measuring the Level of Your Depression

In this section, we provide the Beck Depression Inventory, a questionnaire for you to use in determining whether you are depressed and, if you *are* depressed, the level of your depression.* We would like you to complete this questionnaire right now.

---

*A. T. Beck, *Depression* (New York: Harper & Row [Hoeber Medical Division], 1967), pp. 186–207 and 333–35.

BECK DEPRESSION INVENTORY*

Instructions: This is a questionnaire. On the questionnaire are groups of statements. Please read the entire group of statements in each category. Then pick out the one statement in the group which best describes the way you feel *today,* that is, *right now.* Circle the number beside the statement you have chosen. If several statements in the group seem to apply equally well, circle each one.

    Be sure to read all the statements in the group before making your choice.

A. (SADNESS)
- 0   I do not feel sad
- 1   I feel blue or sad
- 2a I am blue or sad all the time and I can't snap out of it
- 2b I am so sad or unhappy that it is quite painful
- 3   I am so sad or unhappy that I can't stand it

B. (PESSIMISM)
- 0   I am not particularly pessimistic or discouraged about the future
- 1   I feel discouraged about the future
- 2a I feel I have nothing to look forward to
- 2b I feel that I won't ever get over my troubles
- 3   I feel that the future is hopeless and that things cannot improve

C. (SENSE OF FAILURE)
- 0   I do not feel like a failure
- 1   I feel I have failed more than the average person
- 2a I feel I have accomplished very little that is worthwhile or that means anything
- 2b As I look back on my life all I can see is a lot of failure
- 3   I feel I am a complete failure as a person (parent, spouse)

D. (DISSATISFACTION)
- 0   I am not particularly dissatisfied
- 1   I feel bored most of the time
- 2a I don't enjoy things the way I used to
- 2b I don't get satisfaction out of anything any more
- 3   I am dissatisfied with everything

E. (GUILT)
- 0   I don't feel particularly guilty
- 1   I feel bad or unworthy a good part of the time
- 2a I feel quite guilty
- 2b I feel bad or unworthy practically all the time now
- 3   I feel as though I am very bad or worthless

F. (EXPECTATION OF PUNISHMENT)
- 0   I don't feel I am being punished
- 1   I have a feeling that something bad may happen to me
- 2   I feel I am being punished or will be punished
- 3a I feel I deserve to be punished
- 3b I want to be punished

*The authors wish to thank Aaron T. Beck, M.D., for granting permission to reprint the Beck Depression Inventory.

G. (SELF-DISLIKE)
0   I don't feel disappointed in myself
1a I am disappointed in myself
1b I don't like myself
2   I am disgusted with myself
3   I hate myself

H. (SELF-ACCUSATIONS)
0   I don't feel I am worse than any-body else
1   I am critical of myself for my weaknesses or mistakes
2   I blame myself for my faults
3   I blame myself for everything that happens

I. (SUICIDAL IDEAS)
0   I don't have any thoughts of harming myself
1   I have thoughts of harming my-self but I would not carry them out
2a I feel I would be better off dead
2b I feel my family would be better off if I were dead
3a I have definite plans about com-mitting suicide
3b I would kill myself if I could

J. (CRYING)
0   I don't cry any more than usual
1   I cry more than I used to
2   I cry all the time now. I can't stop it
3   I used to be able to cry but now I can't cry at all even though I want to

K. (IRRITABILITY)
0   I am no more irritated now than I ever am
1   I get annoyed or irritated more easily than I used to
2   I feel irritated all the time
3   I don't get irritated at all at things that used to irritate me

L. (SOCIAL WITHDRAWAL)
0   I have not lost interest in other people
1   I am less interested in other peo-ple now than I used to be
2   I have lost most of my interest in other people and have little feel-ing for them
3   I have lost all my interest in other people and don't care about them at all

M. (INDECISIVENESS)
0   I make decisions about as well as ever
1   I try to put off making decisions
2   I have great difficulty in making decisions
3   I can't make any decisions at all anymore

N. (BODY IMAGE CHANGE)
0   I don't feel I look any worse than I used to
1   I am worried that I am looking old or unattractive
2   I feel that there are permanent changes in my appearance and they make me look unattractive
3   I feel that I am ugly or repulsive looking

O. (WORK RETARDATION)
  0   I can work as well as before
  1a It takes extra effort to get started doing something
  1b I don't work as well as I used to
  2   I have to push myself very hard to do anything
  3   I can't do any work at all

Q. (FATIGABILITY)
  0   I don't get any more tired than usual
  1   I get tired more easily than I used to
  2   I get tired from doing nothing
  3   I get too tired to do anything

S. (WEIGHT LOSS)
  0   I haven't lost much weight, if any, lately
  1   I have lost more than 5 pounds
  2   I have lost more than 10 pounds
  3   I have lost more than 15 pounds

U. (LOSS OF LIBIDO)
  0   I have not noticed any recent change in my interest in sex
  1   I am less interested in sex than I used to be
  2   I am much less interested in sex now
  3   I have lost interest in sex completely

P. (INSOMNIA)
  0   I can sleep as well as usual
  1   I wake up more tired in the morning than I used to
  2   I wake up 2–3 hours earlier than usual and find it hard to get back to sleep
  3   I wake up early every day and can't get more than 5 hours' sleep

R. (ANOREXIA)
  0   My appetite is not worse than usual
  1   My appetite is not as good as it used to be
  2   My appetite is much worse now
  3   I have no appetite at all

T. (SOMATIC PREOCCUPATION)
  0   I am no more concerned about my health than usual
  1   I am concerned about aches and pains or upset stomach or constipation
  2   I am so concerned with how I feel or what I feel that it's hard to think of much else
  3   I am completely absorbed in what I feel

To score the questionnaire, just add the points you received from your responses to each item. If you circled more than one response for an item, add *only* the points for the highest response. For example, if in answering item G *(Self-Dislike)* you circled both (3) "I hate myself" and (2) "I am disgusted with myself," add 3 points for that item.

Table 1–1 presents the range of scores for each of four levels of depression. This book is designed primarily for persons whose scores on the Beck Depression Inventory are between 5 and 15.

TABLE 1–1
Beck Depression Inventory—Estimated Degree of Depression

Range of Scores	Depression Level
0–4	None or minimal
5–7	Mild
8–15	Moderate
16 or over	Potentially serious

If your score was between 0 and 4, you are probably not depressed. You may be having some real life difficulties, but depression may not be the best label for what you are experiencing. Conversely, if you scored low and you remain convinced that you are depressed, you may have scored low for at least three reasons:

1. Today may be an unusually good day for you.
2. The test may not include enough of the kinds of ways in which you experience depression.
3. You may not have been depressed lately but know that you have a tendency to become depressed.

If any of the foregoing three reasons are true for you, you still may find this book helpful.

If your score was 16 or higher, we encourage you to give this book a try. If the book seems difficult to get into, then seek professional assistance, as recommended in the next section.

Suggestions for When to Seek Professional Help

If any of the following points apply to you, we suggest that you seek professional assistance through your community mental health clinic, a nearby university department of psychiatry or psychology, a psychologist or psychiatrist in private practice, or your physician:

1. If your score on the Beck Depression Inventory was 16 or higher, indicating potentially serious depression, and, if, after giving this book a try, you don't feel it's going to be helpful.
2. If you are seriously contemplating suicide.
3. If you have been experiencing wide mood swings: feeling very depressed for a while and then feeling abnormally ecstatic, flighty, and full of almost superhuman energy, with virtually no "neutral" time.
4. If, as a result of reading this chapter and taking the Beck Depression Inventory, you have decided that you are not depressed but you continue to experience psychological distress of some kind.

SUMMARY

In this chapter we introduce our definition of depression—first, by saying what depression is *not* (it is not just any upsetting feeling) and then by describing the kinds of feelings and behaviors that have been found to be characteristic of depressed persons as a group. The Beck Depression Inventory was provided so that you could measure your present level of depression. Finally, we gave some guidelines to help you decide whether this book will help you or whether you should seek professional assistance.

REVIEW

☐ I have a reasonably clear idea of what depression is and what it is not.
☐ I have an understanding of the collection of specific feelings and behaviors that make up the depressive syndrome.
☐ I have assessed the level of depression I am currently experiencing.
☐ I have made a preliminary decision:
   ☐ to proceed with reading this book.
   ☐ to seek professional assistance.

2

Social Learning:
A Way to Think About
People's Behavior

Human beings have tried to understand themselves and other people for centuries. There is a strong desire to explain to ourselves why we like certain things and dislike or fear others, why we find it easy to do this and have so much trouble doing that, why we feel good one day and terrible on another. Some people are friendly and enthusiastic whereas others seem grouchy and dull most of the time. Most interestingly, some who are usually boring can blossom into the life of the party, and some who are gruff and stingy can at times be gentle, kind, and generous.

One reason people are interested in why we do the things we do is that we like to know what makes people tick. This is pure intellectual curiosity. Another reason is that we would like our knowledge to be a positive influence on our lives. We'd like to have more of a say about how we feel and what we are likely to do. We'd like to be able to influence others to be more friendly toward us, more cooperative, and more understanding. We'd like to be able to bring up our children in ways that will make them more competent in dealing with life.

Psychology, as a field of study, seeks to understand human behavior—that is, to study why people behave, think, and feel the way they do. Because human behavior is so complex and is influenced by so many factors, there is as yet no single theory that explains it completely. Different psychologists emphasize different factors. The approach we use in therapy is called social learning theory. It is based on what is known about the *learning* process and how *social* factors influence human life.

From a social learning view, people are seen as *learning* almost everything they do. Within the limits set by our physical makeup, the way we walk, talk, eat, sleep, think, and even the way we feel is *learned*. Think, for example, of the way a sailor acquires his "sea legs," or a good mountaineer learns to have sure footing, or, for that matter, the way a baby learns to walk. The way we talk is a clear example of the learning process: Think about how easily we can distinguish a New England accent from a British accent, or a southern drawl from a western twang. The kinds of food we eat vary according to what we have learned to like: Some people find snails disgusting, and others love them; some people think peanut butter is horrible, but others enjoy it.

The *way* we think is a very important but neglected area of study. Some people can understand how numbers work very easily. Others have learned to think about cooking—flavors, colors, texture, nutrition—as though it were second nature to them. Still others have acquired a remarkable facility in thinking about politics, business, religion, puzzles, or mechanics. Just as we learn to do certain things, we learn to think in certain ways: Some persons learn to be more organized, some more intuitive, some more optimistic, some more pessimistic, some more traditional, and some more innovative.

Finally, we learn different ways of feeling. For example, we learn to feel happy when our favorite baseball, football, or hockey team wins and disappointed when it loses, but someone who isn't interested in sports feels nothing at all. We learn to feel sentimental about a certain song after hearing it played when we are with someone "special." We learn to feel safe in our homes and to feel loved when someone we care for smiles at us.

Knowing that people learn to act, think, and feel the way they do, we can say that depression itself is *learned*. Some individuals learn to act, think, and feel in depressing ways. Therefore, the way to control depression is for the depressed person to learn new patterns that make depression less likely. Of course, this is more easily said than done! And that is what this book is designed to do—to give you step-by-step directions, which, if followed, will teach you how to change the way you think and act so that you will feel more alive and less depressed.

We will introduce here a few of the concepts we use throughout the book. The next chapter will help you begin to focus on some specifics about how the social learning approach can help you deal with depression.

What Influences Behavior?

ANTECEDENTS

Antecedents are situations or events that happen *before* the behavior. For example, certain physical situations can increase or decrease the chances that you will feel and act depressed. You are more likely to feel sad and cry when visiting a cemetery than when visiting an amusement park.

A social situation can also act as an antecedent. You are more likely to act businesslike with your boss, happy and active with your dancing class, and sad and helpless with a friend or relative who has repeatedly provided a shoulder for you to cry on.

Places, people, or the time of the day may influence how you'll think, act, and feel. These factors are antecedents in the sense that they set the stage for the outcome of different behaviors from you.

> Alfred, a single man who was in treatment for depression, complained that it was hard for him to meet and develop friendships with women. He said that almost every time he approached a woman, he became doubtful about whether he really wanted to meet her; he then became formal in manner, thinking of the many reasons why she was not suitable for him.
>
> Further discussion of Alfred's problem revealed that he usually visited bars or discos when he was consciously trying to meet women. It was in these bars or discos that he suffered from his uncomfortable doubts, formal behavior, and negative thoughts about the women he saw. When he met women in other places, however, he had no such responses. The antecedents to his discomfort seemed to be the bars and discos and not the actual interactions with females.
>
> Alfred began to keep track of places that brought out his most pleasant moods, spontaneous behavior, and positive thoughts about the women he met. He came up with the following: (1) a courtyard near his office building where many downtown workers ate their bag lunches, (2) jogging meets, especially before a race or a "fun run," and (3) citizen action-group gatherings, especially those concerned with local issues. He found that in these places he could speak to women fairly easily and informally and that, in general, he found them interesting and easy to admire.
>
> He wondered how he had come to associate his uncomfortable feelings with bars and discos and decided that he must have developed some sort of prejudice against them because he went there only when he felt desperate for company. He probably assumed that the women he met there were equally desperate. Whether or not this was the explanation, it was clear that he had positive biases toward the other locations, and he decided to capitalize on them to make his interactions with women more comfortable.

CONSEQUENCES

Consequences are events that follow a behavior. There are positive, negative, and neutral consequences. Positive consequences, or rewards, make it more likely that you'll repeat a behavior. Negative consequences, sometimes called punishment, make it less likely that you'll repeat a behavior.

As you think about the behaviors and thoughts that accompany your depression, you might think about the "payoff"—that is, the positive consequences that follow your behaving in a depressed way.

Holly's parents are very important people in their community. They care very much for Holly, but because of their active schedules, they haven't been able to spend much time with her. She had always understood and even shared the excitement they felt in their roles as community leaders, but there was something nice about how they took more time to be with her when she looked sad or troubled. Holly didn't feel sad frequently, but when she did she was able to have warm, heart-to-heart talks with her parents.

Holly became worried when she started to have periods of sadness more often than before. At first she wondered whether it was just that she was getting older and her worries were more serious, but somehow this explanation was not satisfactory. At the suggestion from a friend of the family, Holly asked her parents to set aside a certain amount of time for her each week, at a regular time. The sad periods soon became less frequent.

What the friend had noticed was that, without intentionally doing so, Holly's parents were teaching her to become sad. They were providing positive consequences each time Holly felt bad and showed it by her depressed expression. The irony in the situation was that, even with the best of intentions, her parents were training Holly to become sad to get attention.

MENTAL FACTORS

Your expectations, beliefs, and other thoughts can greatly influence your activities and your feelings. For example, if you *expect* to have a terrible time at a school get-together, you probably *will*. Thoughts can act as antecedents in the sense that they can "set the stage" for feeling depressed or contented. They also can act as consequences in that you can reinforce or punish yourself with them.

Vince came to one of his therapy sessions quite excited. He had been working on his tendency to be very pessimistic and the relationship between that tendency and his recurring bouts with depression.

Today he felt he had finally found a good explanation for how pessimism helped produce depression. In his opinion, pessimism was telling yourself that something good was not going to happen or that something bad would happen. Now, if you told yourself this when you were about to begin working on something constructive, you would in a sense be punishing yourself for starting the project, and therefore you would be less likely to carry out your plans. You'd get stuck at Step 1. That would mean you wouldn't accomplish what you wanted, and you'd have another reason to be depressed.

According to Vince, pessimism works as a self-fulfilling prophecy, which not only helps you fail, but also increases your chances of becoming depressed because of the failure.

This was a turning point in Vince's treatment. He began to pay close attention to his thoughts and their influence on his behavior. Using techniques like those found in Chapters 9, 10, and 11 of this book, Vince began to set himself up for success, including success in managing depression.

The Connection Between Thoughts, Actions, and Feelings

Our students and our patients have found the following concepts helpful in thinking about depression. The three most important functions that human beings are capable of are thinking, acting (that is, doing), and feeling. These three human functions are inextricably intertwined—that is, they are continually influencing one another.

FEELINGS INFLUENCE ACTIONS

When we talk about depression, we focus primarily on how we *feel*. However, most people who have felt depressed have noticed how *feelings* of depression influence their *activities*. Thus, you may have found yourself doing fewer things when you are depressed, and saying that this is because you "don't *feel* like *doing* anything."

FEELINGS INFLUENCE THOUGHTS

Another thing that people who feel depressed will report is that they can't think of anything positive. It is hard for them to think positive things about themselves, or to think about things that they would enjoy doing, or things they look forward to doing.

On the other hand, they find it too easy to think about negative things. Many depressed people find that they "can't help" thinking about all the work they have to do, their most difficult responsibilities, the negative things that happened in their past, all the problems in today's world, and the many possible tragedies that could happen.

Thus far, we have mentioned how feelings can have an effect on *actions* and thoughts. We could picture this relationship as follows:

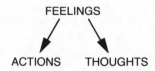

But there is more to the story.

All three of these human functions affect each other all the time. Actions also influence how we feel, and thoughts influence how we feel.

And, of course, actions and thoughts influence each other. A more accurate picture of this relationship looks like this:

ACTIONS INFLUENCE FEELINGS

If you were to sit in an empty room with nothing to do for days, you would soon begin to feel bored, and perhaps angry or depressed. However, if you sat next to your bed and pounded your fist into a pillow, you would begin to feel anger. The act of hitting brings out the feeling of anger.

There is now some evidence that by moving the muscles of the face in ways that are associated with certain feelings, not only can you begin to experience those feelings, but internal biological processes connected with those feelings begin to occur. (The people who advise us to "put a smile on your face" to learn to be happier may have something there!)

THOUGHTS INFLUENCE FEELINGS

Try this experiment: Think of the most embarrassing moment of your life. You will find that you begin to reexperience the feelings of embarrassment that you had back then. You might even find that you are beginning to blush. Obviously, you are not doing anything embarrassing at present. It is the thought alone that is producing the feelings and the physiological reaction (blushing) connected to the feeling.

Now think of something sad. Again, you will find that you begin to experience feelings of sadness. But a moment ago you were experiencing embarrassment! And the only thing that has changed is your thoughts. Nothing has changed in the "real world," yet your thoughts can bring about very different feelings. It is important to realize the power of thoughts, as well as the fact that sometimes it is not what is actually occurring in our lives that influences our feelings of depression, but rather what we are thinking about at the time.

Now focus your thoughts on something enjoyable and relaxing, such as resting, playing, listening to music, and so on. The longer you focus on such thoughts, the more likely you are to begin to feel relaxed.

ACTIONS INFLUENCE THOUGHTS

Let's go back to the pillow-pounding experiment. We had used it to demonstrate that actions can bring out feelings. In this case, pounding the pillow brings out anger. However, along with the feelings of anger, some people also begin to remember specific things that *made* them angry.

Walking into a place of worship may trigger thoughts related to your religion. Going to a supermarket makes one think about the next few meals that one is going to prepare so that the necessary ingredients are purchased.

THOUGHTS INFLUENCE ACTIONS

How thoughts influence actions is perhaps the easiest connection to illustrate:

- It is your memory that in order to get to the office in time you need to leave by 7:00 that influences how fast you rush in the morning.
- It is the thought that if you don't fill up the gas tank your car will stop dead that keeps you looking at the gas gauge periodically.
- It is the thought that you may learn practical ways to better control your mood that keeps you reading this book.

Throughout this book, it is important to remember that what we are doing is giving you strategies that you can use to have better control of your mood. Being told to "feel better" is not very helpful. Most of us find it hard to change our feelings on command. It is easier to change the things we do and the things we think about. Because feelings, thoughts, and actions are so closely connected, we can gain greater control over our mood by changing our thoughts and our actions.

Strategies That Help Self-Change Efforts

The social learning approach is useful not only in understanding why we behave as we do but also in developing effective strategies to change our behavior. You have read about the important influence consequences have on behavior; this knowledge provides a powerful tool you can use in systematically changing your behavior. We call this tool *contracting*.

Contracting means making a specific agreement with yourself to reward yourself *if and only if* you do certain things. The purpose of the contract is to arrange in advance a specific, positive consequence (reinforcement) to follow the achievement of a goal. For example, your contract might state that you will have dinner at your favorite restaurant *if and only if* you complete a particular task.

Why are rewards so important? First, any self-change plan is tedious and difficult to develop and carry out. Second, meaningful change takes effort. Therefore, it is highly desirable for you to incorporate a contract in which you arrange to reinforce yourself for accomplishing your goals.

Reinforcers may involve material rewards, time, or mental events. Examples of material rewards include food, magazines or books, clothes, records, and other objects requiring money. Time could involve earning time to do things you like to do but rarely have time for, such as taking a relaxing bath, sunbathing, talking on the phone, and even "wasting time." Mental rewards can be self-generated "pats on the back" (such as thinking about your good points, your accomplishments, good relationships with others) or mental "treats" (such as daydreaming about pleasurable things, meditating, or listening to music). The items on the Pleasant Events Schedule (Table 6-1) might suggest other reinforcers.

There are four important considerations in selecting a reinforcer.

1. It must be something that is going to make you feel good.

2. It must be accessible to you. You can't go skiing in the summer, and you may not be able to afford a trip to Hawaii.

3. You should be concerned about the strength of the reinforcer. Will you gain enough from the reward to compensate you for the time and effort that it will take to achieve your goal? You should think of the reinforcement as not only rewarding the target behavior but as offering enough reinforcement for your *total* effort.

4. It must be something that you can definitely control. Thus, having your husband take you out to dinner is a reinforcer you might want to select *if* you can count on him to deliver the goods. If you involve other people in your contract, you will probably want to discuss it with them beforehand. There are advantages to involving another person because that mobilizes another motivational factor: social pressure.

You also need to be concerned about the time relationship in writing your contract. Try to make the reinforcement take place as close in time to the achievement of a goal as possible—the sooner, the better. You don't want to reinforce yourself two weeks later. Of course, it may not be practical for you to reinforce yourself immediately, but it's better to do so, especially in the beginning. Perhaps you should reconsider your choice of rewarding events if there is too much of a time delay.

Figure 2-1 shows a model contract which illustrates many of the points we've discussed as being important.

In addition to self-reinforcement through contracting, there are three other concepts from the social learning approach that are especially relevant to self-change efforts:

1. **Step-by-step change:** Slow, deliberate change in working toward goals for behavior change. In its most concrete form, gradual change means increasing or decreasing by *very small steps* the amount of time or the number of times that you perform the target behavior. Self-reward for each successful step is, of course, part of this process.
2. **Modeling:** Learning by observing others. You can use people whom you like and respect, public figures, or even fictional characters as models of the kind of behavior you want to develop and use.
3. **Self-observation:** Noticing and keeping written records of your behavior, thoughts, or feelings. This strategy helps you know better what you are doing *before* you start your self-change program and how much progress you are making as you put the program into effect.

FIGURE 2–1
Model Contract

Required Behavior	If I, *Eleanor Jacobsen,* *go to the Bridge Club on Monday afternoon and to the Obsidian Club on Tuesday evening and if I initiate a conversation at each of these gatherings with someone whom I had not met before,*
Reward	I will reward myself *by spending Wednesday afternoon at the Valley River Shopping Center and try to find and buy a dress I really like.*

Signed,

Eleanor Jacobsen

The Question of Control

People often ask whether we have any control over our feelings or behavior. If we have learned how to act in certain ways during our childhood and if our present environment influences our behavior, how can we change anything? Aren't we at the mercy of our upbringing and our present situation? Other people ask why we have to use rewards, gradual change, self-observation, and so on. Can't we just resolve to change and do it, using willpower? Don't we control our environment, too?

Social learning theory views this problem of control as a chicken-and-egg question. It is true that our environment exerts an influence on us. It is also true that we influence our environment. The process is one of continuous interaction between a person and his or her environment. By learning what factors affect us, we can choose to change them so that they will affect us in a more desirable way.

The changes you make now will become your past history when you look back. You can make your history happen!

Important Implications of Social Learning

1. Early experiences do not necessarily limit your potential. You can always learn new ways of acting, thinking, and feeling.
2. You have a great deal of control over how you change because you can determine what you will and will not reward yourself for from now on.
3. Your expectations can influence how successful you will be in your change efforts. If you are pessimistic, every time you start to implement your change program you are in effect telling yourself: "What's the use, really? It's hopeless." Does that sound encouraging? On the other hand, if you are more optimistic, you are actually telling yourself: "Who knows? Maybe I *can* do it." By being more optimistic, you can increase the chances that you will continue to try and do well.
4. Social learning focuses on the present. You want to know what factors are maintaining your behavior *now* so that you can find out how to modify them. How your behavior patterns got started may be interesting, but at this point it is not necessary to know that to change yourself.

Beware of your avoiding this social learning approach because you find it to be "mechanistic" or "not human enough." It is true that it is systematic—that is what makes it work so well. But so is language. Each letter in a word must be in exactly the right place, and, yet, with those words one can create beautiful poems, songs, and novels! Social learning techniques can increase your personal freedom by allowing you to have many more alternatives from which to choose.

SUMMARY

This chapter introduces the ideas used in this book to deal with depression. The ideas are known as the *social learning approach*. This approach focuses on how people learn to think, act, and feel. It considers antecedents, consequences, and mental factors very important influences on behavior. The chapter describes basic self-control techniques and the implications of using this approach.

REVIEW

- ☐ I understand what the social learning theory is.
- ☐ I have learned about the three main influences on behavior:
  - ☐ antecedents
  - ☐ consequences
  - ☐ mental factors
- ☐ I know the four strategies to bring about self-change:
  - ☐ self-reinforcement
  - ☐ step-by-step change
  - ☐ modeling
  - ☐ self-observation

3

Depression and Social Learning

You may have been feeling depressed for a long time or for only a little while. You may feel depressed often or only occasionally. You may be able to date the onset of your depression to some specific event (your child went to college, you moved to a new city, you retired, you discovered that you had a serious illness such as heart disease, cancer, or arthritis, or someone close to you died), or, on the other hand, you may not be able to recognize any particular event that preceded your depression. Overall, the chances are good that you feel puzzled and don't feel that you understand *why* you get depressed and why you are unable to feel happy again.

The major purpose of this chapter is to present a framework for understanding depression. The critical questions are: What causes people to feel depressed? What causes *you* to feel depressed? How can the social learning framework help you to identify specific behaviors and situations that contribute to your depression? How can the social learning framework help you to control your depression?

A Way to Understand Depression

Except when we are sleeping, we are continuously interacting with our environment. Whether we are watching television, typing a report, talking to a salesperson, interacting with our children or spouse, talking to someone on the telephone, or just sitting and thinking about something from the past—we are always doing something. Our interaction with our environment is continuous.

In a general way we can put our interactions into three groups: those that lead to *positive* outcomes (you finish a task and someone compliments you on it); those that have *neutral* outcomes (you drive to the store); and those that have *negative* outcomes (being criticized by someone who is important to you). When too few of our interactions have positive outcomes and when too many of them have negative outcomes, we start feeling depressed. These routes to depression are shown below.

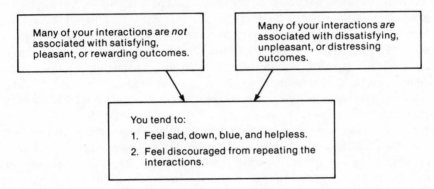

Obviously, not all of our interactions can be expected to lead to positive outcomes; neither is it reasonable to expect that *none* of our actions will lead to negative outcomes. Nevertheless, without a reasonable balance between positive and negative outcomes, it is likely that a person will experience depression.

Here are two examples of interactions which *lack positive* outcomes:

You spend most of your day doing the housework, preparing dinner, waiting for the plumber (who never shows up), and chauffeuring your children to their various appointments. During dinner, your family is busily engaged in discussing their school or job activities, and nobody compliments you on the dinner or inquires about your day. You feel down and begin to wonder whether your family really cares about you. You continue to feel this way for the remainder of the evening and have trouble falling asleep.

You work hard and long on a report requested by your boss. You submit it before the due date, but you never hear about it again. You assume that your boss didn't like it and that you wasted your time.

Here are two examples of interactions associated with *negative* outcomes:

Your wife is critical of you because you come home late from work, read the newspaper during dinner, don't spend enough time with the children, and so on. She complains to you about these things frequently.

At a social gathering you express your opinion about a political candidate. Mrs. X points out that you are "all wrong." You feel stupid and humiliated.

Any one of these situations might leave you feeling a little discouraged but not necessarily depressed. But when these events are multiplied and when they occur over an extended period of time, they are likely to cause you to feel quite depressed.

What determines whether an interaction or a situation is going to be experienced positively or negatively? This depends not only on the actual situation (e.g., your husband compliments you) but also on your interpretation of the situation (e.g., "He didn't really mean it . . ."). What we say to ourselves, especially positive and negative statements, is important. We are said to "self-reinforce" when we provide ourselves with something tangible or when we make a positive statement (e.g., "I handled this situation well") *following* something we do. Self-reinforcement becomes especially important when we are working on projects which require such long and sustained effort that we may not get any encouraging feedback for long periods of time (working on a term paper, doing the annual cleanup of your house, taking a course, or working toward a college degree. The things that you say to yourself while engaged in the activity ("I am doing a good job," "I am making progress," "This may be hard, but the end result is going to be worthwhile,") play a critical role in determining whether a situation is going to be experienced as rewarding or as unpleasant. People who are depressed tend to self-reinforce negatively rather than positively. That is, they are less likely to compliment themselves after they have done something well and are more likely to criticize themselves during or following an activity.

Generally, interactions with positive outcomes are those that make us feel liked, respected, loved, useful, appreciated, and worthwhile. Not only do these interactions make us feel good, but they also cause us to want to be more active. On the other hand, interactions with negative outcomes make us feel bad, unwanted, unappreciated, criticized, and humiliated. Being depressed means that you are experiencing too few positive outcomes and too many negative ones. This state of affairs leads to a vicious cycle: When you feel depressed you also feel discouraged, and are thus less likely to approach situations that might lead to satisfying outcomes. For example, the fact that your comments about a political candidate were rebuffed might make it less likely that you will be motivated to enter the same or similar social situations; the fact that you feel upset about your husband's criticism of you might make it less likely that you will be able to respond to his loving or sexual advances later on.

Vicious and Positive Circles

Everyone knows what a vicious circle is. Picture this scenario: You are in a tight financial situation and need your car to get to work. Your car breaks down, which results in costing you money and making your financial situation even worse. The fact that your car needs repair causes you to miss work, which results in costing you money by reducing your paycheck, which makes it even more difficult for you to get your car fixed—which you need to get to work—which you need to get the money to fix the car, and so on.

With depression, it's rather easy to get into a vicious circle. Having few interactions with positive outcomes causes you to feel depressed; the more depressed you feel, the less motivated you are to engage in the kinds of activities which might have had positive outcomes; this causes you to feel even more depressed, which, in turn, causes you to become even less active. And so it goes on and on. This circle continues until you feel very depressed and are very inactive.

Here is an example of depression as a vicious circle.

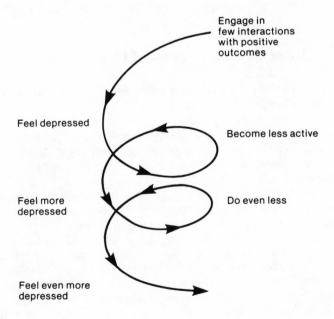

During the past week you have had very few interactions that were followed by positive outcomes. The sale on which you have been spending a lot of time and energy has fallen apart. Your wife has been preoccupied with her mother's poor health and has had little time for you. Your best friend is out of town, and you have been spending a great deal of time by yourself. It is not surprising that you feel somewhat depressed. Consequently, you are finding it more difficult than usual to motivate yourself to do the things that you would normally enjoy: jogging in the morning, making arrangements to go fishing, setting up a luncheon appointment with an acquaintance. You are less likely, therefore, to be in situations or to engage in activities that are usually pleasant for you (i.e., activities with positive outcomes). Consequently, you feel even more depressed and feel even less like doing things.

Fortunately, for every vicious circle there is a *positive* circle:

You decide to go jogging, which makes you feel better. Your wife stops worrying about her mother and returns to being her normal pleasant self in her interactions with you. Consequently, you feel less depressed and feel like making the effort to arrange for a fishing trip or calling a friend about going to lunch.

Engaging in interactions with positive outcomes leads to an improved sense of well-being, which motivates a person to engage in more activities with pleasant outcomes. A positive circle is thus set in motion.

Other Consequences of Depression

When a person has been feeling depressed for a long period of time, a number of things happen:

1. You become pessimistic. You *correctly* perceive that your activities are not associated with positive outcomes. You don't *expect* future activities to lead to positive outcomes. You become less hopeful, and eventually you feel hopeless.
2. You lose interest. You find it more and more difficult to do things, especially those activities requiring effort. If your efforts are not going to lead to positive outcomes, why should you even try?
3. You may begin to wonder whether there is something "wrong" with you. You may start wondering if there is something physically wrong with you, or you may start feeling that you are inferior or inadequate. You may start blaming yourself or wonder whether you are somehow being punished. It seems that there *must* be a reason for your misery.
4. Because you are doing less and less, you may not be meeting your responsibilities. You may be letting other people down. Hence, you start feeling guilty.

Multiple Roads to Depression

How does a person get into this kind of situation? There are many different circumstances in which our interactions may not be followed by positive outcomes. We can think of these as the "causes" of depression.

Interactions that have been a source of positive outcomes for you in the past are no longer available. If you lose, through death or other form of separation, someone with whom you have had many pleasant interactions and with whom you have shared many activities, then that person's departure represents a serious disruption to your usual interactions. Your relationship with the "departed" person may not necessarily have been positive. Most of our relationships have positive *and* negative outcomes. Nevertheless, your inability to interact with that person can represent a serious reduction in the level of positive outcomes you experience. This will probably cause you to feel depressed, at least temporarily. Such things as physical disease, age-related changes, moves to a new city, and serious financial setbacks often reduce our ability to engage in those activities which have been sources of positive outcomes.

Here are some examples of circumstances leading to a reduction of positive outcomes.

You have always been a physically active person and have enjoyed participating in sports and other physically demanding activities. You have recently suffered a heart attack or some other physically disabling disease, and your physician forbids you to engage in many of these activities.

You move to a new city where you don't know anybody. You miss getting together with family and friends in your home town.

Since the recent birth of your first child, you are spending much more time at home. You are less able to meet socially with your friends.

You have been used to playing a lot of golf and tennis and are transferred to a part of the country where the long, hard winter prevents you from participating in these sports.

You may lack the skill to achieve positive outcomes in your interactions. The word *skill* is not easily defined because skills are specific to certain areas or situations. Someone who is an accomplished pianist may not be very good when it comes to fixing his or her lawnmower. By "skill" we are referring to your ability to achieve positive outcomes in situations that are important to you. One particularly important skill in regard to depression is social skill. By this we mean your ability to manage your interpersonal relationships: being able to do the kinds of things that make other people treat you the way you want to be treated. By our definition, you might be said to lack social skill if you are unable to have social interactions which produce the kinds of positive outcomes you enjoy. Many depressed individuals are concerned about their interpersonal relationships. They feel inadequate, uncomfortable, and sometimes disliked and rejected. In other words, social interactions usually do not have positive outcomes for them. Here is an example:

> You like talking with people. There are some particular people you like, and you want them to like you. However, at social gatherings involving more than one or two people, you tend to feel uncomfortable and self-conscious. You and your husband have been invited to dinner at the Franklin home. The dinner is attended by three other couples. You feel tense and ill at ease. Consequently, you don't participate as much as the other persons. Your few efforts to participate in the conversation, although your comments are as good as those of the other people, don't leave you with any feeling of satisfaction because you don't feel that you contributed enough to the conversation. At the end of the evening you feel unhappy and dissatisfied with yourself.

There are other, more subtle skills that influence positive outcomes. One of these has to do with how high we set our standards or goals. In the previous example, if you had expected to be the life of the party, you obviously would not have felt good about your participation. On the other hand, if you had set a more modest goal for yourself, you might have judged your performance more favorably. How we evaluate what we do is determined by the standards we set for ourselves. Getting a pay raise is "objectively" a positive outcome; however, if you expected a much more substantial increase, you may not experience the increase you received to be a positive outcome.

There are other skills important to influencing positive outcomes. You may lack the skills to engage in the kind of occupation you would really enjoy. You may lack the skill to make a successful career change in mid-life. If you have recently retired from work or if your children have grown up and have left home, you may need to develop new skills to allow you to plan your leisure time and to find new activities to replace those that are no longer available to you.

Subtle Ways of Remaining Depressed

Thus far, we have been discussing the direct or immediate causes of depression. For a variety of reasons the depressed person has ended up in circumstances in which his or her activities lead to few positive outcomes and to many negative outcomes. By thinking about yourself carefully, you should be able to evaluate the degree to which your activities and interactions with other people are associated with positive and negative outcomes. Look carefully at the quantity and quality of your interactions. To what extent do they lead to positive outcomes? To what extent do they lead to negative outcomes?

There is another more subtle way in which feelings of depression may occur and continue. A person who is depressed is hurting for good reason. He or she is in real pain. There is a natural tendency to want to tell somebody when we hurt, which undoubtedly goes back to childhood, when we were "reinforced" by our parents or other caring adults for telling them when and where we hurt. They wanted to know because they cared for us and needed to decide if we should see a doctor. Because they needed to know how we hurt in order to protect us, they (our parents, our doctor, and other concerned persons) usually listened to our complaints with interest, sympathy, and understanding. Sometimes just being able to tell someone about your hurts and seeing that they were listening carefully made you feel better. Thus, telling others about our hurts often has a positive outcome. It's natural therefore that an adult who is feeling bad would want to tell someone about it, with the expectation that the other person will listen sympathetically. Talking about your depression and having a sympathetic ear to listen to you may become a positive interaction and may thereby serve to *perpetuate* the depression. As you remember from the previous chapter, interactions with positive outcomes are more likely to be repeated; thus, you may have developed a way of interacting with other people that has the unintended consequence of prolonging your depression. In other words, "talking depression" can become an important source of positive reinforcement and thereby prolongs it.

Mary's husband, Frank, is very preoccupied with his work. At dinner and at other times when they are together they spend a good deal of their time talking about his problems. Mary is genuinely interested in his problems, but there are times when she would also like to discuss some of the things that happen in *her* daily life. Whenever Mary introduces a topic of interest to her, Frank shows only mild interest and quickly returns to *his* topic. Thus, Mary's efforts to have positive interactions with Frank are not very success-ful. In this situation, the interaction is not reciprocal (not in balance) because Frank is not willing to provide Mary with the interest and attention that she is providing him. Since Mary's relationship with her husband is her major source of reinforcement (she doesn't have a job and their children have gone to college), this lack of give and take in their relationship is an important cause of Mary's depression. Mary begins to have trouble sleeping (she has trouble falling asleep and wakes several times in the night) and she doesn't feel rested when she wakes up in the morning. She loses interest in her daily activities, she feels tired, and she finds that it becomes an increasing effort to do anything. Mary is beginning to feel depressed. At the dinner table, she reports her problems with sleeping and her feelings of fatigue to Frank, who becomes unusually interested in her health. He may even inquire about her complaints, how well she has slept, and so on. Unwittingly, Mary has finally found a key to obtaining his interest—which she wants very much! It is likely that she will begin to report her symptoms to him more often.

It's easy to see how some people become "chronic depressives." By becoming especially sympathetic and attentive, friends and relatives often unwittingly reinforce someone talking about one's depression. As time goes on, "talking depression" becomes more frequent and becomes an important part of interactions with others.

Charting Your Daily Mood

The purpose of this book is to help you learn how to cope with your depression and to improve the way you feel. It is very important for you to *look carefully at your activities and interactions* to determine which of your interactions lead to positive outcomes and which lead to negative outcomes. In order to help you feel less depressed, the succeeding chapters will show you how to increase positive outcomes and how to decrease negative ones. To do this you will have to be able to *identify specific instances* from your daily life which have positive and negative outcomes.

The general expectation is that you will feel better on days when you have a lot of positive and few negative interactions. Your knowledge about how you feel or that your mood changes from day to day will be helpful because it will allow you to become aware of the effect of specific events on your mood.

Moods vary from day to day and also from hour to hour. Even people who say they feel depressed "all the time" find that there are days when they feel less unhappy. By keeping track of your daily mood you put yourself in a position to do the following:

1. Identify specific interactions, activities, and situations where you feel especially good or bad.
2. Evaluate your progress toward overcoming your depression.

Because your primary goal is to reduce your depression level, tracking your mood will allow you to evaluate how successful you are in improving it. The Daily Mood Rating Form (Figure 3–1) uses a 9-point scale to help you indicate how good or bad you feel. At the end of each day, about an hour before you go to bed, decide what kind of day it has been for you. If

FIGURE 3–1
Daily Mood Rating Form

Monitoring Day	Date	Mood Score	Monitoring Day	Date	Mood Score
1			16		
2			17		
3			18		
4			19		
5			20		
6			21		
7			22		
8			23		
9			24		
10			25		
11			26		
12			27		
13			28		
14			29		
15			30		

it has been a bad day, you would mark a low number on the chart; if it has been a good day, you would mark a high number. Begin to rate your daily mood *today* and continue to make ratings at the end of each day as long as you are working on any of the chapters of this book. You may wish to monitor your mood after you have succeeded in reducing your depression. In this way the mood ratings can serve as a warning signal if you begin to get depressed again in the future.*

Mary recorded her daily mood score for 30 days, as shown in Figure 3–2. Note that she felt quite depressed during the first week, her mood became more variable (she had some good and some bad days) during the second and third weeks, and she felt good on most days during the fourth week, although she still experienced an occasional bad day. Please rate your mood for today (how good or bad you felt) using the 9-point scale shown. If you felt really great (the best you have ever felt or can imagine yourself feeling), mark 9. If it was a "so-so" (or mixed) day, mark 5. If you

*A copy of the Daily Mood Rating Form is included in the section titled *Extra Forms,* beginning on page 211. You may wish to use it to make additional copies for future daily monitoring of your mood.

FIGURE 3–2
Mary K's Daily Mood Ratings from June 10 to July 9

Monitoring Day	Date	Mood Score	Monitoring Day	Date	Mood Score
1	6-10	3	16	6-25	3
2	11	3	17	26	8
3	12	1	18	27	2
4	13	3	19	28	5
5	14	3	20	29	4
6	15	1	21	30	8
7	16	3	22	7-1	7
8	17	4	23	2	9
9	18	6	24	3	8
10	19	3	25	4	5
11	20	7	26	5	6
12	21	9	27	6	3
13	22	6	28	7	7
14	23	3	29	8	8
15	24	2	30	9	8

felt worse than "so-so," mark a number between 2 and 4. If you felt better than "so-so," mark a number between 6 and 9. Remember, a low number signifies that you felt bad and a high number means that you felt good.

```
        very                                    very
     depressed_____happy
              1  2  3  4  5  6  7  8  9
```

Enter the date on which you begin your mood ratings in Column 2 and your mood score in Column 3.

SUMMARY

The social learning approach to depression attaches primary importance to the quality and quantity of our activities and our interactions with people. When many of our activities are not associated with positive outcomes, we tend to feel depressed. Feeling depressed makes us feel less motivated to be active. Being passive makes it even less likely that we will have interactions with positive outcomes.

There are many reasons why you may be feeling depressed. As a result of major changes in your life situation, many interactions which had been sources of positive outcomes may no longer be available and/or you may lack the skills needed to obtain positive outcomes from your interactions. Therefore, in order for you to reduce your depression, you will need to change the quality and quantity of your interactions in the direction of more positive and fewer negative outcomes. This requires that you look carefully at your activities and interactions to determine which activities lead to positive outcomes and which activities are associated with negative outcomes. The Daily Mood Rating Form will help you to become aware of the specific impact of events on your mood. The daily mood ratings will also allow you to evaluate how successful you are in improving your mood.

REVIEW

☐ I have a general understanding of the social learning approach to depression.

☐ I have begun to examine the quality and the quantity of my daily activities to help me understand why I am feeling depressed.

☐ I have begun to think of reasons why few of my activities have positive outcomes.

☐ I have begun to rate my daily mood using the form in Figure 3–3 and intend to continue making daily mood ratings for at least 30 days.

part two
THE
STRATEGIES

4

Creating a Personal Plan to Overcome Depression

Thus far, you have probably been reading straight through this book. The chapters up to now have provided a general background about depression; reading them was necessary in order to understand and use the rest of this book. But from this point on you may not need to read each chapter. Instead, you may decide to skip around and read chapters out of order to get the best results from this book. There are two reasons for this: First, some of the chapters deal with specific problems which may be of much greater importance to *your* depression; other chapters may not be as directly relevant to you. Second, we want you to tackle no more than one or two problems at a time. After finishing this chapter, you should have a good overview of what is available in the chapters that follow. In addition, you will have *set priorities* in such a way that you will be able to decide which problems you should work on first.

In Chapter 1 you learned that not everyone experiences depression in the same way. Some people will feel guilty and have trouble sleeping and eating when depressed; others will isolate themselves and feel lonely and friendless; still others will cry often and give up their usual pleasant activities.

Every depressed person has a unique set of specific problems. You need to evaluate how *you* experience depression and decide which parts of this book can be of most help to *you*. At this point you may feel eager to read and use everything you can. Every problem we suggest may sound familiar, and you may feel like changing many things about yourself at once. There is a natural tendency for all of us to want many things to change quickly. Unfortunately, this is not realistic. If you try to do too much, you're likely to end up confused, discouraged, and more depressed than ever. You're much more likely to be successful if you focus on a small number of problems that are very important to you. If you do one or two things at a time, you can make progress and feel more self-confident. Then, if you wish, you can try one or two more things and continue to improve yourself. Take it slow; set yourself up for success, not for failure.

This chapter will help you identify the problems you have and determine which of these are related to your depression; it will help you decide how important each problem is. Then you can concentrate on the sections of the book that focus on those problems. We have tried to focus on those problems that are most commonly related to depression. Therefore, not *every* problem experienced by people in life is covered in this book. However, if you are especially concerned about a problem that is not discussed in this book, we have suggested how you can get additional help.

Self-Assessment: Taking Stock of Your Problems

RELAXATION

Do you consider yourself to be a relaxed person or a tense, anxious person? Try to answer not just in terms of whether you know how to relax but also in terms of whether you actually *feel relaxed* most of the time. If you are experiencing any of the following problems, you are probably not feeling relaxed most of the time:

1. If your muscles feel tight, tense, or cramped during the day or if you wake up with muscle cramps during the night, you may be experiencing muscle tension.
2. If you often feel tired and there is no major physical reason for it, it may be that you are wasting energy because your muscles are tight and tense.
3. If you have frequent headaches (more than one or two a week) or if your headaches are very intense, you are probably tensing your facial muscles or the muscles in your neck and shoulders.
4. If you have trouble sleeping, you are probably not relaxing at night. If it normally takes you more than an hour to go to sleep or if you wake up in the night or early morning more than once or twice a week, then you may want to learn how to relax.
5. If you have painful stomachaches more than once or twice a week, it is possible that they are caused by tension (obviously, you should also check out such symptoms with a medical doctor).
6. If you often feel jittery or shaky, then you need to learn to relax.

If you are experiencing any of the problems mentioned here, then you need to learn to relax. For now, if you are experiencing any of the difficulties just described, go to Figure 4–1 on page 57 and write "Relaxation" on the first line under the *Problem* heading. Next to the problem, write "Chapter 5" under the *Chapter* heading. Chapter 5 describes how to relax and how to use relaxation to solve specific problems such as insomnia, headaches, nervous stomach, and so on. Ignore the *Importance* heading for now, and continue evaluating your depression-related problems.

PLEASANT ACTIVITIES

Many people who are depressed stop or drastically cut down on doing things that they used to enjoy. Some people are hardly involved in any activities. Others may be busy doing what they *have* to do, but they have given up the things they *want* to do simply for enjoyment. Consequently, these people feel that the fun has gone out of life and lose hope that anything *could* be much fun. Nothing sounds very pleasant, so there seems to be no reason to try to become active again.

Think about whether any of these things have happened to you. Are you doing as many pleasant things as you used to do before you became depressed? Compared with other people your age, are you doing as many enjoyable things? Are you doing at least a few things each day that are pleasant for you? Is there a balance in your life between getting chores and responsibilities taken care of while still having time for your own interests? If you answered "no" to any of these questions turn to Figure 4–1 on page 57 and write "Pleasant Activities" under the *Problem* heading and "Chapter 6" under the *Chapter* heading. Later you will decide whether this is one of the most important problems for you to work on.

PROBLEMS WITH PEOPLE

Comparing and evaluating your own social behavior is a difficult task. If you are like most people, it is hard to be objective or accurate about your personal attractiveness and social appeal. It may help you to discuss the following questions with someone you know well and trust, rather than trying to judge yourself. Consider the following:

1. Do you have trouble behaving in an assertive manner? All of these skills are part of being appropriately assertive:

–Giving praise or compliments sincerely.
–Saying "no" when you mean it.
–Speaking up when someone asks for your opinion.
–Offering constructive criticism when it would be useful.
–Being able to express anger without blowing up at other people.
–Being able to tell other people about your feelings of love or friendship for them.

Being assertive is a broad category; it includes more than the things listed here. In general, assertion is the ability to express your own thoughts and feelings clearly and directly without imposing them on other people or making other people feel uncomfortable. If you lack skills in doing this, turn to Figure 4–1 on page 57 and write "Social skills: Assertion" under the *Problem* heading and "Chapter 7" under the *Chapter* heading.

2. Is your style pleasant or unpleasant to those around you? Are people comfortable with you or do you have mannerisms and behavior habits that make other people uncomfortable? Some unpleasant mannerisms that depressed people often develop are listed here:

–Slow, halting speech.
–Criticizing others.
–Lack of responsiveness (not answering questions, not taking your turn in a conversation, and so on).
–Ignoring other people.
–Not showing interest in what other people say.
–Lack of eye contact while talking to other people.
–Focusing on negative things in your speech, complaining, brooding out loud, and so on.
–Lack of good grooming.
–Unpleasant facial expression (frowns, scowls).

If you have acquired any of these negative personal habits you may find that people avoid you or are prevented from enjoying your company. This knowledge may make you even more depressed than you already are. If you are experiencing any of the problems listed, write "Social skills: Personal style" under the *Problem* heading and "Chapter 7" under the *Chapter* heading on the chart in Figure 4–1 (page 57).

3. Do you spend very little of your time doing things with other people? People who are depressed tend to be socially isolated or lose interest in being with friends. Even if they are around people, they often stop interacting and don't make an effort to get to know other persons better; they stop making plans to do pleasant things with other people.

Think about the following questions:

1. Are you spending less time with people than you did before you became depressed?
2. Do you feel that you spend less time with people than others do?
3. Have you stopped getting together with friends?
4. When you are with a group of friends, have you started sitting by yourself in silence rather than talking to your friends?
5. Do you feel cut off from old friends as a result of moving to a new area or a new place to live?

If any of these things are happening to you, this is likely to be a significant problem area. If you have answered "yes" to any of these questions, write "Social skills: Isolation" under the *Problem* heading and "Chapter 8" under the *Chapter* heading in Figure 4–1 (page 57).

There are many different kinds of social problems. If you feel this is a problem area for you but none of the specific problems described here seem to fit, there are several things you can do. You might skim Chapters 7 and 8 to see whether the material covered there addresses your particular problem. It it does, enter "Social skills" under the *Problem* heading and write the appropriate chapter number next to it in Figure 4–1. Later you can decide whether to begin with that problem or whether it is less important than other areas.

If the problems you have are not covered in Chapters 7 or 8 or if they seem to be related to interpersonal problems in your marriage or at work, continue to read this chapter. The evaluation of marital and vocational problems will be discussed toward the end of this chapter.

Some social problems may not be covered in this book at all, such as severe conflicts with one particular person (such as a neighbor or a parent) or problems with impulsive or explosive anger. If one of these is an important problem for you, it might be a good idea to talk to a counselor. Such a talk may help you decide whether you need to seek help for your social problems or whether there are other life problems that need to be tackled first.

TROUBLESOME THOUGHTS

Often people who are depressed have a number of negative, self-critical, or pessimistic thoughts. In fact, it is hard to imagine that anyone who is usually thinking about happy or pleasant things could be depressed. Think about the following questions:

1. Do you have unpleasant, negative thoughts whenever your attention is not completely directed?
2. Do you find yourself expecting negative outcomes and worrying about them even when there's insufficient reason to think something bad might happen?
3. Do you sometimes (as often as once a day) think about something that seems really horrible to you?
4. Are you upset because you don't seem able to turn off your negative, self-critical, or pessimistic thoughts?

If you answered "yes" to any of these questions, then learning how to control your thoughts will be helpful to you. Write "Controlling thoughts" under the *Problem* heading and "Chapter 9" next to it on the chart in Figure 4–1 on page 57.

APPROACHING YOUR PROBLEMS CONSTRUCTIVELY

Another problem depressed people often face is an inability to react in a reasonable or constructive way when they run into a problem. Think about your own reaction to difficulties:

1. Do you overreact to upsetting events and find it difficult to cope with problems?
2. Do you tend to think of yourself as a victim of problems rather than tackling the problems by trying to solve them?
3. Do you feel that it is shameful to have problems or that you are worthless if you run into a difficulty?

You may recognize yourself in these statements or the situations may sound familiar to you, even though the statements may not be phrased exactly the way you might express them. If you are having a problem in being able to approach your problems constructively, write "Constructive approach" under the *Problem* heading and "Chapter 10" under the *Chapter* heading next to it on the chart in Figure 4–1 (page 57). Later you will decide whether this is one of the most important problems you face right now.

SELF-CONTROL PROBLEMS

Helping yourself is difficult. This book assumes that you are able and willing to work on your own to change some of your life problems. You *are* willing. The fact that you have gotten this far shows that you are interested. However, you will soon have to start working very hard and follow through on your plans. For depressed people this is often a difficult thing to do. When people become depressed, they often feel tired, passive, easily discouraged, and ready to quit. It's not easy to keep going when you feel lousy. But you will *need* to keep going, even when it's difficult in order to start feeling good about yourself. In order to tell whether you might find it especially difficult to keep working on your problems, think about the following questions:

1. Have you tried a self-help program before and then given up on it?
2. Do you "freeze" in difficult situations and let things get out of hand? (That is, do you find that you know what you should do but wind up not doing it for some reason?)
3. Do you start things—like dieting or giving up smoking—and then drop them because you have lost interest?
4. Do you have a number of half-finished projects lying around at home or at work?

If you answered "yes" to any of these questions, you may need to master self-control skills before you begin to work on other specific problems. If you need to develop better self-control, write "Self-Control" under the *Problem* heading and "Chapter 11" under the *Chapter* heading in Figure 4–1 on page 57. If you decide to list this particular problem, you should *immediately* mark a number 1 in the left-hand column titled *Importance*. You will need to be able to make a sustained effort in order to solve any other problems you have already listed.

Problems Related to Depression But Not Covered in This Book

MARITAL PROBLEMS

This book does not attempt to help you resolve major marital problems, although some of your marital difficulties may be helped by reading this book. For instance, if your mate wants you to be more active and do more things that are enjoyable rather than sitting around so much, then working on Chapter 6 *(Pleasant Activities)* may help your marriage at the same time that it helps you personally. However, most serious marital problems are complex, and you should think about getting professional help for them.

There are four qualities we feel a good marriage should have. If your marriage does not provide the satisfactions discussed in the following list, you may want to talk with your mate about marital counseling. The next section, *Seeking Help for Marital Problems*, will describe some procedures for finding a counselor in your area. (By "counselor" we mean a counseling or clinical psychologist, marriage and family counselor, clinical social worker, or other trained professional.)

1. In a good marriage, partners share pleasant activities together. They don't spend *all* their time together, of course, but they do often take time to do things that are mutually pleasurable. If you and your spouse spend very little time together or if most of your time together is spent on daily, routine chores, you might want to explore together what activities you could begin sharing. You might be able to do this on your own, but it might be a better idea to find a counselor who could help you.

2. In a good marriage, there is a reasonable level of conflict. It is normal for disagreements to occur, but disagreements can be worked out in a good marriage without extreme anger or prolonged conflict. If you fight frequently or fight with a great deal of bitterness, you might want to seek help from a marriage counselor.

3. In a good marriage, the couple's sexual relationship is a source of mutual satisfaction. Sex may be frequent or infrequent, partners may be creative or satisfied with a routine, and orgasm may or may not occur every time there is sexual contact. The specific details of the sexual relationship vary tremendously among good marriages, but in good relationships, the partners agree about sex and enjoy the sexual relationship they have worked out together. If this is not true of your marriage, then you may wish to seek help for this problem. Be sure to read the next section, *Seeking Help for Marital Problems*, carefully if you are selecting a counselor for help with sexual problems; not all counselors are trained to deal with sexual difficulties.

4. In a good marriage, there is almost always a close, intimate relationship in which partners have mutual goals and plans. Marriage partners let each other know very private, personal thoughts and feelings. They feel free to seek help from each other, share their fears and disappointments, and decide together about how to handle problems that arise. Certainly it is not imperative to share *everything* with your partner or reveal all your private thoughts, but a good marriage is usually an intimate relationship, and marital intimacy arises out of a willingness to reveal yourself to your partner. If this is not true in your marriage, you may wish to seek help in order to change your relationship.

Seeking Help for Marital Problems. We suggested in Chapter 1 that professional help could be sought through your community mental health clinic, a nearby university department of psychiatry or psychology, a psychologist or psychiatrist in private practice, or your family doctor. Those suggestions also apply to seeking help for marital problems, but a few additional suggestions may be helpful. First, you might begin by calling your local mental health center and asking whether it has a family counseling service division. Second, when contacting any of these resources, be sure to specify that you want help for *marital problems* and that you would like help *as a couple*, rather than individual therapy. Third, some competent counselors may be available in your area who do not fit into the categories we have outlined. For instance, there might be a good counseling department at a university close to you with counselors available who specialize in family problems. Some universities train social workers and offer family counseling as part of that training, or there might be social workers at a state or local agency who could help you.

If you and your partner have sexual problems, you need to be especially careful in selecting a professional therapist. Sexual counseling is a relatively new field, and there are a number of unqualified people calling themselves sex therapists who have "jumped on the bandwagon" without adequate training. To receive qualified counseling, you should probably follow the recommendations of your community mental health center or contact a nearby university with a department of psychiatry or a graduate department of psychology.

Additional self-help books that might supplement this one are listed at the end of this book. Included are several books dealing with marital and sexual problems; one of these may be useful to you.

VOCATIONAL PROBLEMS

Many people become depressed because they are experiencing great dissatisfaction with their job or educational plans. Dissatisfaction can be caused by any number of problems, ranging from dislike of a particular co-worker to boredom and frustration about the meaning or importance of one's work. Women who have been housewives may feel frustrated or bored. Many men and women in midlife (40s and 50s) experience a letdown when they feel that their work is no longer as challenging or interesting as it once was. Dissatisfaction is often increased by the feeling that there are no alternatives and that nothing will ever change. If you don't know what other job options you have, don't know about training programs available, or don't realize what skills you might already have, it is hard to know what choices are open to you so that you are able to achieve greater satisfaction from your work.

Luckily, there are things you can do to find out about work alternatives. Most community or junior colleges have vocational counseling available to anyone living in the area; usually this is provided free or for a nominal charge. You can easily call and find out whether such a service is available in your area. In addition, many communities have vocational rehabilitation programs available; your local mental health center would know about programs in your area. If you check into these resources, you will discover that there are *always* alternatives to an unsatisfying job. That discovery may be the first step to overcoming your depression. It is possible that just *considering* alternatives and knowing you have choices will help. This can give you a greater sense of control, and you may decide that what you have is better than the alternatives or that you can make changes within your present job. Or you may decide that you really do need a change. Either way, the fact that you have considered alternatives may give you a new sense of freedom and responsibility.

ALCOHOL AND DRUG PROBLEMS

It is not uncommon for people who are depressed to abuse alcohol or other drugs. The problems can be related in numerous ways. Sometimes people begin using alcohol or other drugs when they become depressed because they want to feel better. Other people may become depressed as a result of their excessive use of alcohol or other drugs. Undoubtedly, there are also cases where the two problems (depression and drug use) develop independently, but having both of these problems makes it very difficult to solve either one.

Most people whose use of alcohol or other drugs interferes with their lives are unwilling to admit that they *have* a problem. Thus, your self-evaluation of whether you have a drug or alcohol problem is unlikely to be accurate or objective. If you are depressed and you drink or use drugs even moderately, you should seek out someone who will be honest with you and talk to that person about your use of alcohol or other drugs. Then make a decision about whether you need to seek professional help. One book that may be helpful to you if you have a drinking problem is *How to Control Your Drinking*, by William R. Miller and Ricardo F. Muñoz.* Alcohol and drug problems can be solved, and there is nothing shameful about admitting your need for help. If you are depressed and abusing alcohol or other drugs, it is *essential* that you find the strength to seek the help you need.

Physical Problems

People who are depressed often have physical problems. Some of these physical problems have been mentioned already, such as feeling tired all the time, or having headaches or bad stomachaches. If you have these physical problems—or any others—you should definitely see a physician and listen to the advice given. Depression can be the first sign that you are ill, and you almost certainly cannot make a good diagnosis about your own health. If medical treatment is advised, follow through on it and see what effect the treatment has on your depression. If your doctor says you are healthy and that your physical problems are caused by your depression, then listen to that advice, too. Sometimes it's hard to believe that stomachaches or headaches, and other physical problems, are caused by your behavior and emotions, but they can be. If this is the case for you, we urge you to keep working on overcoming your depression, either by using this book or by seeking a counselor. Chapter 5, *Learning to Relax*, may be particularly helpful in dealing with many of your physical ailments.

---

*W. R. Miller and R. F. Muñoz, *How to Control Your Drinking*, Revised edition (Albuquerque: University of New Mexico Press, 1982).

SLEEP PROBLEMS

Problems in sleeping deserve special attention because so many depressed people have trouble sleeping. Some people have difficulty getting to sleep, others wake up too early in the morning, and still others want to sleep all the time during the day but can't fall asleep at night. Our advice for these problems is the same as for other physical problems: First, see a physician to find out whether you have a medical problem. Be careful, however, that you do not hastily accept sleeping medication as the solution to your problem. Sometimes physicians prescribe sleeping pills without clearly establishing that a medical or physiological problem exists and without realizing that these medications actually disturb sleep patterns when used on a prolonged basis. If you do have a sleeping problem, you will probably want to work on it as part of overcoming your depression. Chapter 5 may be helpful. You may also want to read *How to Sleep Better*, by Thomas Coates and Carl Thoresen.*

Where Should You Start?

At this point, you have a list of problems you want to tackle (Figure 4–1). To this list add any major problems you have identified which are not covered in the subsequent chapters of this book. Be sure to include marital problems, work or school problems, and alcohol or other drug problems as one of these additional major problems if they apply. Next to each, under the *Chapter* heading, write "Professional help" or "Other self-help book," since those problems will not be covered in this book.

The next step is to decide where to begin; remember that you should work on only one or two problems at a time. If self-control is on your list, you already know the first problem you must solve. Similarly, if you have indicated that you have a problem with alcohol or other drugs, it would be wise to deal with that problem first and return to this book when your alcohol or drug abuse is under control. In all other cases. you will have to decide where you wish to start.

Under the *Importance* heading, number the problems you have, beginning with number 1 for the most important and working through the entire list. The following guidelines may help if you are having difficulty making decisions about the relative importance of each problem.

---

*T. J. Coates and C. E. Thoresen, *How to Sleep Better* (Englewood Cliffs, N.J.: Prentice-Hall, 1977).

1. Try not to equate "Importance" with "Difficulty of Changing." That is, don't resolve to tackle all the hardest problems first just because you know how difficult they are to change. For instance, learning to relax or finding an hour a day to engage in pleasant activities may be relatively easy changes for you, but they may be very *important* in overcoming your depression. In fact, you will feel much better if you start with some problems that are relatively easy to solve and really matter to you. Then, when you are feeling better, you can tackle some of the more complicated or difficult problems. On the other hand, don't start with easy problems if you know they are trivial; if you do, you will exhaust your initial enthusiasm about changing before you really get to anything important.
2. If nothing stands out as more important than other problems, we suggest that you begin with Chapter 6, *Pleasant Activities.* Being able to have fun is important for depressed people; increasing pleasant activities usually leads to a positive change in mood and increased energy for tackling difficulties.
3. You can always change your mind, so don't get too worried about which problems are most important. If you start on a problem and find that you can't resolve it until you work on something else, just change your plan. For example, imagine that you started out by trying to work on increasing pleasant activities but found you were always tired because you weren't sleeping at night. In this case you would just switch the order of the problems you work on; work on relaxation and sleep, and then return to pleasant activities when you find you are getting more rest. Allow yourself to experiment a little; you can always change your plan!

After you have numbered the problems, you are ready to begin. Now you can start working on the first or second problem listed using either this book, professional help, or some other self-help book. Once you have made significant progress on the first few problems listed, you can work down the list, in order of importance. Thus, occasionally you may set this book aside for a while to work on problems using a different resource, but you can always return to this book when you are ready to tackle a problem that is discussed here. Keep working down your problem list as far as you wish. If you feel fine after solving the first two problems, that's wonderful! You may not want to go further. Most people, however, will probably need to work out several problems before they feel satisfied with the positive changes in their depression. You are the best judge of how much you will need to do.

After you have worked on the problems on your list, we urge you to finish by reading all of the final section of the book, Part III, which gives you some ideas about how to *maintain* your gains, how to *adapt* to future changes, and how to *plan* a self-determined purpose for your life. It is important to read and use Part III, regardless of what problems you work on first and how many problems are on your list.

FIGURE 4-1

Importance	Problem	Chapter

SUMMARY

You are now facing a major, and exciting, task. You began this book feeling depressed and probably confused about your feelings of depression. Now you understand more about depression and social learning. You also have pinpointed some specific problems related to your feelings of depression. Finally, you have a tentative plan for tackling those problems, and you are about to begin carrying out that plan.

You have already made considerable progress, and you should be very pleased with the efforts you have made. You will still need to work hard to keep making progress, but you are off to a good start. We hope you continue to be successful. If you do not succeed, remember that failure with this book does not mean you are a hopeless case. It only means that this method did not work for you, and you will need to find another kind of help in order to overcome your depression.

REVIEW

☐ I now know that I should tackle only one or two problems at a time in order to overcome my depression.

☐ I have listed the problems which seem to be most clearly related to my depression.

☐ I have decided on the order in which I shall work on my problems.

☐ I have decided which chapters from this book I shall use.

☐ I have decided to seek a counselor or use another self-help book for help with problems that are not covered in this book.

5

Learning to Relax

Malcolm is a 45-year-old man who has been depressed for the last five or six weeks. He has also been feeling very tense much of the time and, for the first time in his life, has had trouble falling asleep; lately he tosses and turns for at least two hours before finally drifting off.

Malcolm blames his tension and sleeping problems on his increased job responsibilities. He was promoted to the position of office manager at his company a couple of months ago. He was very happy to receive this promotion and wants to prove that he can do a good job. But the new position is full of pressures, and he finds himself worrying about it most of the time. When he first began having trouble falling asleep, Malcolm went to see his physician. The doctor said that his physical health was good and, fortunately, discouraged him from taking any sleeping pills; instead, he urged Malcolm to find ways to relax. Unfortunately, however, his doctor didn't offer any specific suggestions on how Malcolm could relax; hence, Malcolm has continued his daily routine of intense work, worrying about his performance, and feeling more and more tense and discouraged.

Barbara is a 36-year-old woman who, since adolescence, has had a problem with frequent headaches. Lately her headaches have become more frequent and more severe. Like Malcolm, Barbara consulted her physician; he pronounced her to be in good physical health. When the headaches occur, Barbara takes aspirin, although it doesn't seem to help very much. When Barbara gets a headache, the only thing she feels like doing is taking a nap or watching TV. Therefore, she has been spending more and more time at home and doing fewer of the things she used to find enjoyable.

Phyllis is a 66-year-old woman who, with her husband, recently retired and moved to a new community. Phyllis feels lonely and isolated in her new community; she misses her old friends. She had always been able to get along well with other people. In her former job she enjoyed comfortable friendships with several of her co-workers, and she had been an active, well-liked member of several social and service clubs in her community. In her new neighborhood Phyllis was initially friendly and warm toward a number of people but was disappointed that her attempts at friendship were not more successful. As time went on, Phyllis found that she was often nervous when talking with others, especially if she was in a group of people. She joined a service club in the new town, but at the first meeting she was so tense and fearful that she hardly said anything. She didn't go back to the club and persuaded her husband to turn down some social invitations from people he had met. Phyllis couldn't understand why she was so anxious when she had always been relaxed and easygoing in social situations in the past. She knew her social isolation and loneliness were part of the reason that she felt so depressed, but somehow she couldn't force herself to relate to people in her new community.

Malcolm, Barbara, and Phyllis, despite their different situations, have one thing in common: All three are experiencing some tension-related problems accompanied by depression. As we pointed out in Chapter 1, people who are depressed often also have problems with anxiety or tension. For many, the anxiety of tension contributes directly or indirectly to their feelings of depression. Phyllis, for example, knows her depression is due in part to her feelings of social isolation in her new community. Yet because she feels so fearful and tense in social situations, she avoids them and has become even more socially isolated. Malcolm worries a lot about his new job responsibilities; his tension makes it difficult to fall asleep at night. Getting less sleep and feeling tense so much of the time probably makes him feel quite fatigued and, therefore, less effective in his job. Like Malcolm, Barbara, and Phyllis, you may find yourself caught in this kind of vicious circle where tension-related problems are not only problems in their own right (like Malcolm's sleep problems and Barbara's headaches) but also make it more difficult to do the kinds of things that might help you overcome your depression.

Collecting Some Information First

In this chapter we will present a well-tested and quite simple method for learning to relax. First, though, it will be helpful to collect some base-line data on how tense you are each day and how frequently you experience tension-related symptoms. By keeping records each day for one week, you will be able to accomplish two important steps:

1. You will have a base level against which you can compare your progress as you learn to relax more.
2. You will be able to identify particular situations and/or times of the day when you are most tense.

First, you need to establish a scale to measure how tense you are. We suggest that you use the scale on the Daily Relaxation Monitoring Form (Figure 5–1). On this scale, a 10 represents the most tense or anxious you have been and a 0 represents the most relaxed you have ever been. Malcolm decided that the most tense he could remember being (a 10) was when he was being interviewed for his new job; he remembers feeling most relaxed after swimming while on vacation the previous summer (a 0). For Barbara, her 10 was a few years ago when her young son did not return home and she was afraid he had been injured or was lost; she remembers feeling most relaxed when she was sunbathing at her family's beach cabin. Write down at the top of Figure 5–1 what 10 and 0 are for you, and then for practice rate how relaxed you are *right now*.

Each day you should write three scores on Figure 5–1:

1. Your average relaxation score for the day (how relaxed you felt most of the day that day).
2. The relaxation score for when you felt the *least* relaxed during the day. Also, be sure to note the time, where you were, and a brief description of what you were doing when you felt least relaxed.
3. The relaxation score for when you felt the *most* relaxed during the day. Again, be sure to record the time, the location, and a brief description of what you were doing when you felt relaxed.

In addition to recording these three scores each day, be sure to keep track of any specific tension-related symptom you experience each time it occurs. (Figure 5–1 lists some symbols you can use.) If you have a tension-related physical problem such as headaches or stomachaches, it will also be helpful to note the time at which the symptoms occurred, where you were, and what you were doing. For the first week, just leave the section labeled *Relaxation Practice* blank.

Some samples from Malcolm's and Barbara's daily monitoring for a single day are shown in Figure 5–2.

ONE WORD OF CAUTION: Don't expect this method—or *any* method—to result in getting an average rating of 0 or 1 every day or even to attain a 0 as your most relaxed rating *most* days. That would be an unrealistic goal for anyone. Furthermore, it wouldn't be desirable for most people to be *that* totally relaxed all day every day. Studies have shown that for many kinds of tasks there is a desirable level of tension somewhere between total relaxation and high tension. If Malcolm became so relaxed that he consistently rated himself 0 or 1 while on the job, he probably would get fired because he wouldn't be very productive. A more appropriate goal for Malcolm might be somewhere between 3 and 6 while he is at work. At that level, Malcolm would feel considerably calmer than he does now and would be able to work quite effectively. When he is not

FIGURE 5–1
Daily Relaxation Monitoring Form

Relaxation Rating: 0 = Most relaxed you have ever been
10 = Most tense you have ever been

Date: _____ to _____

	Monday	Tuesday	Wednesday	Thursday	Friday	Saturday	Sunday	Average Score (add your scores and divide by 7)
Average Score for the Day..........								☐
Least Relaxed Time								
Score..........								☐
When..........								
Where..........								
Situation..........								
Most Relaxed Time								
Score..........								☐
When..........								
Where..........								
Situation..........								
Occurrence of Tension Symptoms.......... H = Headache SA = Stomachache SP = Sleep problem								
Relaxation Practice								
When..........								
For how long..........								
Score before..........								☐
Score after..........								☐

FIGURE 5–2
Sample Daily Monitoring Record

Malcolm	Barbara
Average Score 7	Average Score 6
Least Relaxed	Least Relaxed
Score 8	Score 7
When .... *Late morning*	When .... *8–9 a.m.*
Where .... *Office*	Where .... *Home*
Situation .... *Turning down Joe's request for salary increase*	Situation .... *Trying to settle kid's argument*
Most Relaxed	Most Relaxed
Score 4	Score 3
When .... *5–6 P.M.*	When .... *Early evening*
Where .... *Home*	Where .... *Park*
Situation .... *Having drink and reading newspaper*	Situation .... *Taking dog for walk*
Occurrence of Tension	Occurrence of Tension
Symptoms .... *(SP)*	Symptoms ...... *(H) In morning when kids were bickering (H) In late afternoon cooking dinner*

Symbols for tension-related symptoms: (SP) —sleep problem
(SA) —stomachache
(H) —headache

working, it would be good if he could average around 2 or 3 with an occasional 0 and 1 for his most relaxed times.

Learning to Relax

After a week of collecting base-level data, you should begin practicing the relaxation method we will describe in this section.

Learning to relax is in some ways similar to learning any new skill—like tennis, cooking, or oil painting. It takes regular practice, patience, and time. With regular practice, you can soon control your bodily tension and experience a greater degree of relaxation more of the time. Although there are many effective ways to learn to relax (e.g., strenuous exercise, deep muscle relaxation, yoga, and transcendental meditation), we believe that the simplest method, and the one that seems to be suited to nearly everybody, is the relaxation technique developed by Dr. Herbert Benson. His book *The Relaxation Response* is well worth reading, particularly if you are interested in learning about the physiological changes that occur in conjunction with relaxation.* The method described here is based on Dr. Benson's technique. There are five preliminary steps:

1. Choose a quiet, comfortable environment where there are few distractions and where you won't be disturbed by other people.
2. Choose a time of the day when you are least likely to be disturbed by other people and when you won't be worried about having to get somewhere or do something right after your practice session. Dr. Benson suggests that you not hold practice sessions within two hours after a meal because the digestive process may interfere with the relaxation response.
3. Choose a word or phrase to repeat, either silently or aloud, while you are practicing your relaxation. This exercise of repetition is important because it helps prevent your mind from wandering during the practice session. Dr. Benson suggests using the word *one*. But any simple word or phrase will do; we recommend that you choose one that is pleasing to you.
4. Develop a passive attitude while practicing. Don't worry about how well you are performing because that kind of self-evaluation will prevent the relaxation response from occurring. Also, don't worry if you begin to experience distracting thoughts. They will occur for almost everybody. When you become aware of distracting thoughts, simply return to repeating your special word or phrase. Dr. Benson writes that keeping a passive or "let-it-happen" attitude seems to be the most important element in being able to become deeply relaxed.

*H. Benson, *The Relaxation Response* (New York: Avon Books, 1975).

5. Select a comfortable position. This is important in order to prevent muscle tension. Sitting in a comfortable position on your bed or in a soft chair is probably the best choice. Lying down is another good position and one you might like to try later on. However, people tend to fall asleep when they lie down to practice relaxation. If you happen to fall asleep during a practice session, this is a good indication that you are relaxed! But it's impossible to practice while you are asleep. Therefore, we recommend that you begin your practice sessions in a comfortable sitting position.

Those are the preliminaries. The procedure itself is very simple. There are five steps:

1. Sit quietly in a comfortable position.
2. Close your eyes.
3. Relax all your muscles as fully and deeply as possible. You can start with your foot muscles and progress up to your facial muscles. Or start by relaxing your facial muscles and then relax your shoulder and arm muscles, your chest and stomach muscles, your leg muscles, and end with your foot muscles.*
4. Breathe easily and naturally through your nose. *Become aware of your breathing.* As you breath out, say "one" or your special word or phrase, either silenly to yourself or aloud. For example, breathe *in . . .* then *out,* say "one," *in . . . out,* say "one," and so on.
5. Continue for ten to twenty minutes. Open your eyes to check the time, if you wish, but do not set an alarm. When you finish, sit quietly for several minutes, at first keeping your eyes closed; after a minute or so, open your eyes. Remain sitting for several minutes.

We recommend that you practice this method from ten to twenty minutes *once or twice each day,* preferably at a regular time and place. Don't be concerned if your progress seems slow; becoming tense or worried about relaxing is, of course, not very relaxing! As long as you work at the procedure and practice conscientiously, you will gradually experience an enjoyable state of relaxation. The secret is *not* to try too hard.

COMMON PROBLEMS

One of the most frequent problems people have with this procedure is the occurrence of distracting thoughts. As we noted previously, don't worry if your mind wanders during your practice sessions, and don't feel that

---

*Gerald Rosen, *The Relaxation Book* (Englewood Cliffs, N.J.: Prentice-Hall, 1977). This book presents an easy-to-follow procedure for systematically reducing muscle tension.

having distracting thoughts means that you have failed. Instead, simply redirect your attention to your breathing and to repeating your word or phrase.

Another problem people experience is external distraction. Make an effort to prevent this problem by carefully selecting a time and place where you won't be disturbed. After a while you will be able to tolerate some distractions. In the beginning, though, try to find a time that is totally quiet for you.

Some people feel that they are losing control as they "float" into a state of relaxation. If you are uneasy with this feeling, you might want to approach the practice sessions at a slower pace, simply sitting quietly for several minutes before you begin repeating your special word or phrase and concentrating on your breathing. With practice, you will eventually see that *you* are the real director of what you feel, and that you can *control* how relaxed you want to be. If you doubt this, try this experiment in one of your practice sessions: During the middle portion of your session, purposely open your eyes and tense up your muscles. Doing this should convince you that you are in charge!

A number of miscellaneous physical reactions or sensations may occur while you practice relaxation. At times, you may experience small muscle spasms or jerks while you relax. Or you may experience tingling sensations in your muscles or a feeling of floating in your head. These reactions are not unusual and, in fact, are signals that you are *succeeding* in relaxing. With further practice, these reactions either will diminish or will become very familiar and not bothersome to you.

Finally, as is true for learning any new skill, consistent practice is very important. Most people who have learned to relax using this method look forward to their relaxation sessions each day. But at first, practicing may seem like a chore, and you might find yourself coming up with all sorts of excuses for skipping a practice session. If this happens, we suggest that you refer back to Chapter 2. Carefully read the section on contracting and rewarding yourself, and use the suggestions there to set up a self-reward plan for regularly practicing the relaxation method.

Recording Your Practice Sessions

Continue to complete Figure 5–1 each day. You may wish to use the Daily Monitoring Relaxation Form at the end of this book to make additional copies for your use in successive weeks. At the bottom of the form is a place for you to record your daily relaxation practice sessions. For each session, note the time and how long you practiced. Then, using the same relaxation scales as before (0—very relaxed; 10—very tense), rate how relaxed you were immediately *before* the practice session and immediately *after* the session. At the end of each week, look back over your ratings to see if your practice sessions have improved your relaxation. Again, don't worry if your progress seems slow at first. If you continue to be dissatisfied, experiment by choosing a different time or place for your practice sessions, or try a different position.

Applying the Relaxation Procedure to Specific Situations

After you have practiced the relaxation technique for at least a week or ten sessions, you can begin adapting it to your particular problem situation. This step will require some creativity on your part. While you are experimenting, be sure to continue your regular practice sessions at your usual time in your usual place.

The first step in making specific applications is to decide when might be the most effective time to use the relaxation technique. For some people, this decision will be relatively simple. Malcolm, for example, has problems falling asleep at night, so a logical time for him to use the relaxation technique would be just before he goes to bed. For other kinds of problems, the decision may be more complex. One aid in making this decision is to examine your daily monitoring forms to see if there is a clear pattern to your tension. Try to identify particular times of the day or particular situations when you feel most tense. Then try to schedule practice sessions *before* these high-tension times. It may not be possible to hold your usual practice sessions at these times, but see if you can use some modified version of the technique to do them *in addition to* your regular relaxation sessions. Some examples will help illustrate alternatives.

Malcolm: In addition to his problem in falling asleep, Malcolm initially felt very tense most of the time. Practicing relaxation each evening had helped him reduce his tension level and he was able to fall asleep more easily. However, he realized that he was still feeling quite tense at work. His daily monitoring record showed that for the past three weeks his "least relaxed" time on most days had occurred at work. Malcolm decided to get up twenty minutes earlier on weekday mornings in order to have a regular practice session before going to work. After several days of doing this, he was pleased to find that he felt much calmer at work, especially in the morning. To extend this calmness, Malcolm decided to try a modified version of the technique at lunchtime. It was not possible to get the kind of privacy and quiet he needed in his office, so he started to delay eating his lunch by fifteen minutes and used the first part of his lunch hour to sit in his car and practice the relaxation method for ten minutes. He found that although he was not able to become as completely relaxed as he did during his regular relaxation sessions, the five or ten minutes of relaxing in his car helped him to be less tense during the afternoon. Later on, Malcolm was able to relax adequately in his office by simply closing his door and asking not to be disturbed for five minutes. Then, even though there were more distractions and less time, he could regain some of the calm sense of relaxation that he felt during his regular sessions.

Barbara: Having faithfully practiced her relaxation each morning before the rest of her family got up, Barbara found that she was more relaxed and had fewer headaches. At times, though, she still developed headaches in the late afternoon as she began preparing dinner for the family. Because her children were around and because she needed to begin cooking dinner at that hour, it was not practical for Barbara to take twenty minutes for relaxation. However, she *could* take ten or fifteen minutes right before the children got home from school to practice the relaxation technique. She began to schedule two relaxation sessions each day: her usual pre-breakfast session and a shorter mid-afternoon session.

Phyllis: Phyllis had been faithfully practicing the relaxation method for about three weeks. She usually practiced in the morning before breakfast and had found that she felt calmer in the mornings. She began to feel more comfortable chatting with people in her neighborhood, although she still felt anxious about being in a group of strangers. Yet, she did want to become more actively involved in community affairs again. Finally, Phyllis worked up her courage and returned to the service club. Before leaving for the meeting, she held a special relaxation session at home and found that she felt reasonably relaxed. About halfway through the meeting, however, she noticed that she was beginning to tense up. She knew she might become even more tense if she stood up and excused herself. So she stayed where she was, took a deep breath, and relaxed her muscles the way she did at the beginning of her relaxation sessions. She also repeated her special word to herself a couple of times. She was pleased to find that using this "mini" relaxation method helped her feel calmer, and she could do it without anyone noticing her.

These examples are intended to show the need for being flexible and creative in applying the relaxation procedure to your specific situation. Again, it is important that you continue your usual relaxation sessions while doing this kind of experimentation. It is unlikely that modified versions will produce the same degree of relaxation that you can achieve—with practice—in your regular relaxation sessions. Creative use of modified versions, however, can help you feel less tense at those times when you particularly need to feel more relaxed.

We have stressed the importance of scheduling your regular relaxation sessions or doing modified versions of the relaxation method immediately before tension-producing situations occur. We think this is the most effective approach because you can make yourself feel more relaxed before your tension builds up too much. Sometimes, though, you may not be able to have a relaxation session right before a tension-producing situation occurs. Or, even if you *are* able to have a session, you may still find yourself becoming tense once you're in the situation. If and when this happens, we suggest that you try a trick like Phyllis used. There are all kinds of things people can do to help reduce their tension without anyone else noticing. Here are some suggestions:

1. Take a deep breath and focus on your breathing for a couple of minutes.
2. Say "one" or your special word to yourself for a couple of minutes.
3. Picture yourself relaxing in your favorite place.
4. Relax the muscles that feel the most tense. People vary in terms of which muscles are the most tense or tightest for them; for some, it's the hands; for others, the shoulders or back; for still others, the facial muscles. You probably are aware of where you feel the most tense. Focus on relaxing those muscles.

Try one of these methods or a combination of them and see if they help you reduce your tension. Experiment to see what works best for you, and then use that method the next time you find yourself becoming tense.

Evaluating Your Progress

At this point you should have at least two weeks of daily monitoring data entered on the form in Figure 5–1. In the previous section we suggested that you examine your daily monitoring forms in order to identify particular times in your day or particular situations that seem to produce the most tension. When you have identified these situations, write them down in Figure 5–3. When you write them down, avoid making them too specific (e.g., turning down Joe's request for a salary increase) or too general (e.g., turning down requests). Ideally, the problem situations you list should strike a good balance between being specific and general (for example, dealing with employees' requests). To broaden your list or to get some ideas on describing situations that are problems for you, you may want to refer to the Pleasant Events Schedule (Table 6–1 on page 77), the Assertion Questionnaire (Table 7–1 on page 110), or the Social Activities Questionnaire (Table 8–1 on page 127). Again, you will probably want to make copies of Figure 5–3 after you have listed the situations that are tension-producing for you. Then, for each day and for each situation that occurred, rate the degree of your relaxation in that situation. Be sure to rate every occasion on which the situation occurred; this could happen more than once on some days. A rating of 10 indicates that you were very uncomfortable and tense. A rating of 0 indicates that you were completely relaxed and comfortable.

FIGURE 5–3
Daily Relaxation Monitoring for Problem Situations

Relaxation Rating: 0 = Most relaxed you have ever been
10 = Most tense you have ever been

Dates: _____ to _____

Problem Situations	Monday	Tuesday	Wednesday	Thursday	Friday	Saturday	Sunday
1.							
2.							
3.							
4.							
5.							
6.							
7.							
8.							
9.							
10.							

Figure 5–4 is a sample sheet from Phyllis' daily monitoring for a single day.

Note that Phyllis jotted down the names of people or brief comments for some of her activities. She did this so she could clearly remember the situations. You may find this helpful, also.

FIGURE 5–4
Phyllis' Daily Monitoring

Problem Situations

1. Initiating a conversation with a stranger .... 5 *(man at store)*

2. Talking with a co-worker .... 4 *(Sam)*

3. Joining the rest of the group at coffee break .. 8 *(Judi)*

4. Introducing myself to someone .... 7 *(new girl at office)*

5. Inviting an acquaintance to join me for some
   social activity ....

6. Accepting a social invitation ....

7. Going to a service or social club meeting ....

8. Inviting a neighbor over for coffee .... 6 *(Sally)*

From now on, complete *both* Figure 5–1 *and* Figure 5–3 every day.* You can change your list of problem situations on Figure 5–3 as time goes by. In fact, you should review what you have entered in Figure 5–3 each week to make sure it includes the situations that are *currently* the most tension-producing for you. At the end of each week, compare the average relaxation scores on Figure 5–3 with those from the previous week. If you are dissatisfied with your progress, consider how you are applying the relaxation procedure. Are you still having a regular relaxation session at least once a day? Would it be a good idea to change the time and/or place of this session? Are there some new ways in which you could apply modified versions that continue to be tension-producing for you? How about trying some of the "on-the-spot" techniques we suggested? Equally important, are you expecting too much too fast? Remember that changing the way you respond in some problem situations is going to take some time, lots of patience, and faithful practice.

Remember to continue having regular relaxation sessions in addition

*So that you can make additional copies of them, these forms appear in the section titled *Extra Forms*, beginning on page 211.

to practicing any tension-reducing modifications you have found useful. Learning to stay more relaxed can make a big difference in overcoming your depression!

SUMMARY

This chapter was written especially for people whose tension-related problems (such as feeling very anxious in certain social situations, having frequent headaches, or having trouble sleeping) may contribute to their depression. A method of learning the skill of relaxation was presented along with suggestions for applying the relaxation technique in specific problem situations.

REVIEW

☐ In order to collect base-line information on my tension level, I filled out Figure 5–1 every day for one week and then continued to complete this daily monitoring form so I could evaluate my progress.

☐ I learned the relaxation technique presented in this chapter (or another technique that I have found helpful) and have been practicing relaxation in regular sessions each day.

☐ On the basis of my daily monitoring on Figure 5–1, I identified the kinds of situations or times of day when I felt most tense, and, using Figure 5–3, I have kept track of how relaxed I felt in these situations each day.

☐ I have developed a modified version of the relaxation technique and have been using it to help me feel more relaxed in tension-producing situations.

☐ I have evaluated my progress (at least once) by:
   ☐ Figuring my average relaxation score on Figure 5–1 for each week and comparing it with my average score for the previous week.
   ☐ Comparing my ratings (on Figure 5–3) of how relaxed I am in my particular problem situations each week with my ratings from the previous week.

☐ On the basis of my evaluation, I have decided I am:
   ☐ Not presently satisfied with my progress and need to:
      ☐ Continue holding regular practice sessions at least once a day (perhaps finding a better time and place in which to practice).
      ☐ Develop or change my modified versions of the relaxation technique to use immediately before tension-producing situations occur.
      ☐ Try some of the "on-the-spot" techniques suggested for reducing tension when I find that I am in a tension-producing situation.
   ☐ Satisfied with the progress I am making, so I will go on to a different chapter. However, I will continue to:
      ☐ Practice relaxing each day.
      ☐ Use the modified versions of the relaxation method and "on-the-spot" techniques that I've found helpful in reducing my tension.

6

Pleasant Activities

If you feel depressed, it is very likely that you are not involved in many pleasant activities. Or perhaps you *are* involved in activities and don't derive much pleasure from them. The purpose of this chapter is to assist you in the following:

1. Assessing the degree to which the number of pleasant activities and the extent to which you are enjoying them may be contributing to your depression.
2. Developing and carrying out a self-change plan aimed at increasing the number of pleasant activities in which you are involved.

The Relationship Between Pleasant Activities and Depression

When we experience very few activities that we consider to be pleasant, we feel depressed. Also, when we feel depressed, we don't feel like doing the kinds of activities that are likely to be a source of pleasure and satisfaction for us. These are very important facts, and, because of their simplicity, they are often not given the attention they deserve.

There is a chicken-and-egg problem that intrigues psychologists: Does a *low number* of pleasant activities *cause* us to feel depressed, or does *feeling depressed* cause us to be inactive? The answer is likely to be that it works both ways—being involved in only a few pleasant activities causes us to feel depressed *and* being depressed causes us to be inactive. One can think of this as a vicious circle. The less we do, the more depressed we feel; the more depressed we feel, the less we feel like doing anything. We feel trapped in a downward spiral. Fortunately, there is also a positive circle. The more we do, the less depressed we feel; and the less depressed we feel, the more we will feel encouraged to do things.

The fact that there is a relationship between the number of pleasant activities and our mood provides us with a potential "handle" on depression. By increasing pleasant activities, we can make ourselves feel better. Similarly, by maintaining a reasonable level of pleasant activity, we can avoid becoming depressed. In other words, we shift from being controlled by our depression to being able to control it.

Before discussing the practical application of this relationship between pleasant activities and our mood, we need to clarify several questions:

1. What types of activities or events are likely to be experienced as pleasant?
2. What is a reasonable number of pleasant activities to have?

What Kinds of Activities Are Likely to Be Experienced as Pleasant?

Several years ago, we began a series of studies aimed at identifying a comprehensive list of activities that had been pleasant experiences for many people. We were interested in learning something about the nature of such activities and the degree to which people resemble each other in the kinds of activities they enjoy. Perhaps most importantly, we were looking for those activities that had the greatest impact on mood level.

We began by asking persons of all ages to list 10 activities that they had experienced and had found pleasant. This resulted in the "Pleasant Events Schedule" (PES), a list of 320 potentially pleasant activities. It is reproduced in this book as Table 6–1 on page 77. Inspection of this list reveals the wide range of activities that are potentially pleasant for many people. Since then, we have had literally thousands of persons tell us how often they are involved in these activities during a 30-day period, and how much enjoyment they derive from them. Along with monitoring their daily activities, our participants have also monitored their daily mood. From these studies, we have been able to draw the following conclusions:

People differ markedly in regard to the specific kinds of activities they experience as pleasant. Each one of us has his or her own set of potentially pleasant activities. In a very real sense, each of us must discover for ourselves which activities are pleasant for us. In order to identify activities that are potentially pleasant, relevant, and meaningful to a particular person, the first step consists of having the person describe them. Interestingly, the nature of the activities that are a source of pleasure does not change very much as we get older. So, as soon as we know what kinds of activities are pleasant for us, we have discovered something very basic about ourselves.

Some activities are especially important in regard to depression. When our participants engaged in certain activities, they felt good; when they did not, they were more likely to feel depressed. Because this is significant, these activities have been starred in Table 6–1. We refer to them as "mood-related activities," and they fall into three basic groups:

1. Social interactions in which the person feels wanted, liked, respected, understood, appreciated, and accepted (e.g, being with happy people, having people show interest in what you have said, thinking about people you like, being with friends).
2. Activities that make us feel useful, capable, and independent (e.g., doing a project in your own way, planning or organizing something, doing a job well, learning to do something new).
3. Activities that are "intrinsically pleasant" (e.g., laughing, being relaxed, eating good meals, thinking about something good that will happen in the future, seeing beautiful scenery, having peace and quiet, sleeping soundly at night). These kinds of activities are usually accompanied by emotions that are incompatible with being depressed. For example, it is impossible to laugh and to be depressed at the same time.

In general, then, there are three kinds of activities that are especially important in combatting depression: (1) those that involve us in pleasant and meaningful interactions with other people; (2) those that make us feel more competent and adequate and give us a sense of direction and purpose; and (3) those associated with emotions that are the opposite of being depressed.

Developing a Self-Change Plan

By completing the "Pleasant Events Schedule" in Table 6–1, on page 77, you will be able to evaluate the number of pleasant activities in which you are involved. This form will also assist you in finding specific activities you wish to do more often as part of your self-change plan. Begin by taking the test that appears on the following pages. After you have answered the questions, you will become more aware of the many possible pleasant activities available to you which you may not do often enough.

It will take you about two hours to take and score this test. You should plan to take the test in a quiet place and at a time when you will not be interrupted. Because taking the test will require a considerable effort on your part, it's a good idea to plan to reward yourself after you have finished. Decide *now* what kind of a reward you are going to give to yourself after you have finished taking and scoring this test. Before you complete the "Pleasant Events Schedule" read the following very carefully.

HOW OFTEN HAVE THESE EVENTS HAPPENED IN YOUR LIFE IN THE PAST MONTH?

Please answer this question by rating each item on the Frequency Scale (Column F):

> 0—This has *not* happened in the past 30 days.
> 1—This has happened a *few times* (1 to 6 times) in the past 30 days.
> 2—This has happened *often* (7 times or more) in the past 30 days.

Place your rating for each item in Column F. Here is an example:

Item 1 is *Being in the country.* Suppose you have been in the country 3 times during the past 30 days. Then you would mark a 1 in Column F next to Item 1.

Some items will list *more than one event;* for these items, mark how often you have done *any* of the listed events. For example, Item 12 is *Doing artwork (painting, sculpture, drawing, movie-making, and so on).* You should rate Item 12 on how often you have done *any* form of artwork in the past month.

Because this list contains events that might happen to a wide variety of people, you may find that many of the events have not happened to you in the past 30 days. It is not expected that anyone will have done all of these activities in a single month.

Begin now by putting your frequency rating for each of the 320 items in Column F. After you have gone through the list for the first time and have assigned a frequency rating to each of the 320 items, review the list once again. This time ask yourself the following question:

HOW PLEASANT, ENJOYABLE, OR REWARDING WAS EACH EVENT DURING THE PAST MONTH?

Please answer this question by rating each event on the Pleasantness Scale (Column P).

> 0—This was *not* pleasant (use this rating for those events that were either neutral or unpleasant).
> 1—This was *somewhat* pleasant (use this rating for events that were mildly or moderately pleasant).
> 2—This was *very* pleasant (use this rating for events that were strongly or extremely pleasant).

If a particular event has happened to you *more than once* in the past month, try to rate roughly how pleasant it was *on the average*. If an event *has not happened* to you during the past month, then rate it according to how much fun you think it would have been.

When an item lists more than one event, rate it on the events *you have actually done*. (If you haven't done any of the events in such an item, give it the average rating of the events in that item that you would have liked to have done.)

Place your rating for each event in Column P (pleasantness).

Example: Item 1 is *Being in the country*. Suppose that each time you were in the country in the past 30 days you enjoyed it a great deal. You would then rate this event 2 because it was very pleasant.

The list of items may contain some events that you would not enjoy. Keep in mind that the list was made for a wide variety of people, and it is not expected that one person would enjoy all of the activities listed. Go through the entire list rating each event on *roughly how pleasant it was* (or would have been) *during the past 30 days*. Please be sure that you rate each item.

TABLE 6–1
Pleasant Events Schedule

	F	P	$F \times P$	$\sqrt{}$[a]
*1. Being in the country				
2. Wearing expensive or formal clothes				
3. Making contributions to religious, charitable, or other groups				
4. Talking about sports				
*5. Meeting someone new of the same sex.				
6. Taking tests when well prepared				
7. Going to a rock concert				
8. Playing baseball or softball				
*9. Planning trips or vacations				
10. Buying things for myself				
11. Being at the beach				
12. Doing artwork (painting, sculpture, drawing, movie-making, etc.)				

a Use this column to check items for your activity schedule.
* Starred items are mood-related items.

Pleasant Events Schedule *(cont.)*

		F	P	F×P	√[a]
13.	Rock climbing or mountaineering				
14.	Reading the Scriptures or other sacred works				
15.	Playing golf				
16.	Taking part in military activities				
17.	Rearranging or redecorating my room or house				
18.	Going naked				
19.	Going to a sports event				
20.	Reading a "How to Do It" book or article				
21.	Going to the races (horse, car, boat, etc)				
*22.	Reading stories, novels, nonfiction poems, or plays				
23.	Going to a bar, tavern, club, etc.				
24.	Going to lectures or hearing speakers				
*25.	Driving skillfully				
*26.	Breathing clean air				
27.	Thinking up or arranging a song or music				
28.	Getting drunk				
*29.	Saying something clearly				
30.	Boating (canoeing, kayaking, motor-boating, sailing, etc.)				
31.	Pleasing my parents				
32.	Restoring antiques, refinishing furniture, etc.				
33.	Watching TV				
34.	Talking to myself				
35.	Camping				
36.	Working in politics				
37.	Working on machines (cars, bikes, motorcycles, tractors, etc.)				

a Use this column to check items for your Activity Schedule.
* Starred items are mood-related activities.

Pleasant Events Schedule *(cont.)*

	F	P	F×P	√a
*38. Thinking about something good in the future				
39. Playing cards				
40. Completing a difficult task				
*41. Laughing				
42. Solving a problem, puzzle, crossword, etc.				
43. Being at weddings, baptisms, confirmations, etc.				
44. Criticizing someone				
45. Shaving				
46. Having lunch with friends or associates				
47. Taking powerful drugs				
48. Playing tennis				
49. Taking a shower				
50. Driving long distances				
51. Woodworking, carpentry				
52. Writing stories, novels, plays, or poetry				
*53. Being with animals				
54. Riding in an airplane				
55. Exploring (hiking away from known routes, spelunking, etc.)				
*56. Having a frank and open conversation				
57. Singing in a group				
58. Thinking about myself or my problems				
59. Working on my job				
*60. Going to a party				
61. Going to church functions (socials, classes, bazaars, etc.)				
62. Speaking a foreign language				

a Use this column to check items for your Activity Schedule.
* Starred items are mood-related activities.

Pleasant Events Schedule *(cont.)*

	F	P	F×P	√a
63. Going to service, civic, or social club meetings				
64. Going to a business meeting or a convention				
65. Being in a sporty or expensive car				
66. Playing a musical instrument				
67. Making snacks				
68. Snow skiing				
69. Being helped				
*70. Wearing informal clothes				
71. Combing or brushing my hair				
72. Acting				
73. Taking a nap				
*74. Being with friends				
75. Canning, freezing, making preserves, etc.				
76. Driving fast				
77. Solving a personal problem				
78. Being in a city				
79. Taking a bath				
80. Singing to myself				
81. Making food or crafts to sell or give away				
82. Playing pool or billiards				
83. Being with my grandchildren				
84. Playing chess or checkers				
85. Doing craft work (pottery, jewelry, leather, beads, weaving, etc.)				
86. Weighing myself				
87. Scratching myself				
88. Putting on makeup, fixing my hair, etc.				

a Use this column to check items for your Activity Schedule.
* Starred items are mood-related activities.

Pleasant Events Schedule *(cont.)*

	F	P	$F \times P$	$\sqrt{ }$ a
89. Designing or drafting				
90. Visiting people who are sick, shut in, or in trouble				
91. Cheering, rooting				
92. Bowling				
*93. Being popular at a gathering				
*94. Watching wild animals				
95. Having an original idea				
96. Gardening, landscaping, or doing yard work				
97. Shoplifting				
98. Reading essays or technical, academic, or professional literature				
99. Wearing new clothes				
100. Dancing				
*101. Sitting in the sun				
102. Riding a motorcycle				
103. Just sitting and thinking				
104. Social drinking				
*105. Seeing good things happen to my family or friends				
106. Going to a fair, carnival, circus, zoo, or amusement park				
107. Talking about philosophy or religion				
108. Gambling				
*109. Planning or organizing something				
110. Smoking marijuana				
111. Having a drink by myself				
112. Listening to the sounds of nature				

a Use this column to check items for your Activity Schedule.
* Starred items are mood-related activities.

Pleasant Events Schedule *(cont.)*

	F	P	F × P	√a
113. Dating, courting, etc.				
*114. Having a lively talk				
115. Racing in a car, motorcycle, boat, etc.				
116. Listening to the radio				
*117. Having friends come to visit				
118. Playing in a sporting competition				
119. Introducing people I think would like each other				
120. Giving gifts				
121. Going to school or government meetings, court sessions, etc.				
122. Getting massages or backrubs				
123. Getting letters, cards, or notes				
124. Watching the sky, clouds, or a storm				
125. Going on outings (to the park, a picnic, a barbecue, etc.)				
126. Playing basketball				
127. Buying something for my family				
128. Photography				
129. Giving a speech or lecture				
130. Reading maps				
131. Gathering natural objects (wild foods or fruit, rocks, driftwood, etc.)				
132. Working on my finances				
*133. Wearing clean clothes				
134. Making a major purchase or investment (car, appliance, house, stocks, etc.)				
135. Helping someone				
136. Being in the mountains				

a Use this column to check items for your Activity Schedule.
* Starred items are mood-related activities.

Pleasant Events Schedule *(cont.)*   *F*   *P*   *F* × *P*   √ ᵃ

137. Getting a job advancement (being promoted, given a raise, or offered a better job; getting accepted to a better school, etc.)

138. Hearing jokes

139. Winning a bet

140. Talking about my children or grandchildren

141. Meeting someone new of the opposite sex

142. Going to a revival or crusade

143. Talking about my health

*144. Seeing beautiful scenery

*145. Eating good meals

146. Improving my health (having my teeth fixed, getting new glasses, changing my diet, etc.)

147. Being downtown

148. Wrestling or boxing

149. Hunting or shooting

150. Playing in a musical group

151. Hiking

152. Going to a museum or exhibit

153. Writing papers, essays, articles, reports, memos, etc.

*154. Doing a job well

*155. Having spare time

156. Fishing

157. Loaning something

*158. Being noticed as sexually attractive

159. Pleasing employers, teachers, etc.

160. Counseling someone

a Use this column to check items for your Activity Schedule.
* Starred items are mood-related activities.

Pleasant Events Schedule *(cont.)*

	F	P	F×P	√[a]
161. Going to a health club, sauna bath, etc.				
162. Having someone criticize me				
*163. Learning to do something new				
164. Going to a "drive-in" (Dairy Queen, McDonald's, etc.)				
*165. Complimenting or praising someone				
*166. Thinking about people I like				
167. Being at a fraternity or sorority				
168. Taking revenge on someone				
169. Being with my parents				
170. Horseback riding				
171. Protesting social, political, or environmental conditions				
172. Talking on the telephone				
173. Having daydreams				
174. Kicking leaves, sand, pebbles, etc.				
175. Playing lawn sports (badminton, croquet, shuffleboard, horseshoes, etc.)				
176. Going to school reunions, alumni meetings, etc.				
177. Seeing famous people				
178. Going to the movies				
*179. Kissing				
180. Being alone				
181. Budgeting my time				
182. Cooking meals				
183. Being praised by people I admire				
184. Outwitting a "superior"				
*185. Feeling the presence of the Lord in my life				

a Use this column to check items for your Activity Schedule.
* Starred items are mood-related activities.

Pleasant Events Schedule *(cont.)*

	F	P	F × P	√a
*186. Doing a project in my own way				
187. Doing "odd jobs" around the house				
188. Crying				
189. Being told I am needed				
190. Being at a family reunion or get-together				
191. Giving a party or get-together				
192. Washing my hair				
193. Coaching someone				
194. Going to a restaurant				
195. Seeing or smelling a flower or plant				
196. Being invited out				
197. Receiving honors (civic, military, etc.)				
198. Using cologne, perfume, or aftershave				
199. Having someone agree with me				
200. Reminiscing, talking about old times				
201. Getting up early in the morning				
*202. Having peace and quiet				
203. Doing experiments or other scientific work				
204. Visiting friends				
205. Writing in a diary				
206. Playing football				
207. Being counseled				
208. Saying prayers				
209. Giving massages or backrubs				
210. Hitchhiking				
211. Meditating or doing yoga				
212. Seeing a fight				

a Use this column to check items for your Activity Schedule.
* Starred items are mood-related activities.

Pleasant Events Schedule *(cont.)*

	F	P	F×P	√[a]
213. Doing favors for people				
214. Talking with people on the job or in class				
*215. Being relaxed				
216. Being asked for my help or advice				
217. Thinking about other people's problems				
218. Playing board games (Monopoly, Scrabble, etc.)				
*219. Sleeping soundly at night				
220. Doing heavy outdoor work (cutting or chopping wood, clearing land, farm work, etc.)				
221. Reading the newspaper				
222. Shocking people, swearing, making obscene gestures, etc.				
223. Snowmobiling or dune-buggy riding				
224. Being in a body-awareness, sensitivity, encounter, therapy, or "rap" group				
225. Dreaming at night				
226. Playing Ping-Pong				
227. Brushing my teeth				
228. Swimming				
229. Being in a fight				
230. Running, jogging, or doing gymnastics, fitness, or field exercises				
231. Walking barefoot				
232. Playing frisbee or catch				
233. Doing housework or laundry; cleaning things				
234. Being with my roommate				
235. Listening to music				
236. Arguing				

a Use this column to check items for your Activity Schedule.
* Starred items are mood-related activities.

Pleasant Events Schedule *(cont.)*

	F	P	F × P	√ a
237. Knitting, crocheting, embroidery, or fancy needlework				
*238. Petting, necking				
*239. Amusing people				
240. Talking about sex				
241. Going to a barber or beautician				
242. Having house guests				
*243. Being with someone I love				
244. Reading magazines				
245. Sleeping late				
246. Starting a new project				
247. Being stubborn				
*248. Having sexual relations				
249. Having other sexual satisfactions				
250. Going to the library				
251. Playing soccer, rugby, hockey, lacrosse, etc.				
252. Preparing a new or special food				
253. Birdwatching				
254. Shopping				
*255. Watching people				
256. Building or watching a fire				
257. Winning an argument				
258. Selling or trading something				
259. Finishing a project or task				
260. Confessing or apologizing				
261. Repairing things				
262. Working with others as a team				

a Use this column to check items for your Activity Schedule.
* Starred items are mood-related activities.

Pleasant Events Schedule *(cont.)*

	F	P	F × P	√a
263. Bicycling				
264. Telling people what to do				
*265. Being with happy people				
266. Playing party games				
267. Writing letters, cards, or notes				
268. Talking about politics or public affairs				
269. Asking for help or advice				
270. Going to banquets, luncheons, potlucks, etc.				
271. Talking about my hobby or special interest				
272. Watching attractive women or men				
*273. Smiling at people				
274. Playing in sand, a stream, the grass, etc.				
275. Talking about other people				
276. Being with my husband or wife				
*277. Having people show interest in what I have said				
278. Going on field trips, nature walks, etc.				
*279. Expressing my love to someone				
280. Smoking tobacco				
281. Caring for houseplants				
*282. Having coffee, tea, a coke, etc., with friends				
283. Taking a walk				
284. Collecting things				
285. Playing handball, paddleball, squash, etc.				
286. Sewing				
287. Suffering for a good cause				
288. Remembering a departed friend or loved one, visiting the cemetery				
289. Doing things with children				

a Use this column to check items for your Activity Schedule.
* Starred items are mood-related activities.

Pleasant Events Schedule *(cont.)*

	F	P	F×P	√a

290. Beachcombing

*291. Being complimented or told I have done well

*292. Being told I am loved

293. Eating snacks

294. Staying up late

295. Having family members or friends do something that makes me proud of them

296. Being with my children

297. Going to auctions, garage sales, etc.

298. Thinking about an interesting question

299. Doing volunteer work, working on community service projects

300. Water skiing, surfing, scuba diving

301. Receiving money

302. Defending or protecting someone; stopping fraud or abuse

303. Hearing a good sermon

304. Picking up a hitchhiker

305. Winning a competition

306. Making a new friend

307. Talking about my job or school

308. Reading cartoons, comic strips, or comic books

309. Borrowing something

310. Traveling with a group

*311. Seeing old friends

312. Teaching someone

313. Using my strength

314. Traveling

a Use this column to check items for your Activity Schedule.
* Starred items are mood-related activities.

Pleasant Events Schedule *(cont.)*

	F	P	F × P	√ᵃ

315. Going to office parties or departmental get-togethers

316. Attending a concert, opera, or ballet

317. Playing with pets

318. Going to a play

319. Looking at the stars or moon

320. Being coached

a Use this column to check items for your Activity Schedule.
* Starred items are mood-related activities.

TABLE 6–2

	Average Ranges		
Age Group	Mean Frequency Score	Mean Pleasantness Score	Mean Cross-Product Score
20–39	0.63–1.03	0.86–1.26	0.99–1.19
40–59	0.57–0.97	0.82–1.22	0.92–1.12
60 or older	0.50–0.90	0.78–1.18	0.86–1.06

After you have rated each item on frequency and pleasantness, you are ready to do some easy computations that will allow you to assess your rate of pleasant activities.

1. Add the frequency ratings (in Column F) and divide the total by 320. This is your *mean frequency score.* For example, suppose adding all your frequency ratings gives you a total of 176. Dividing this total by 320 equals 0.55. Your mean frequency score tells you something about how much (or how little) you engage in the activities on the list. It reflects your overall activity level. By comparing your score with the average range for persons your age, shown in Table 6–2, you can evaluate yourself. If your score is equal to or lower than the low end of the average range, you are not engaging in the activities to the extent that people your age do.

2. Add the pleasantness ratings (in Column P) and divide the total by 320. For example, if your rating total was 256, you would obtain 0.80 for your *mean pleasantness rating.* The mean pleasantness rating tells you something about your current *potential* for pleasurable experiences. If this number is low (equal to or lower than the low end of the average range shown in Table 6–2), it means that, at present, there are few activities that are sources of satisfaction and pleasure for you. If the score is high,

it means that you have a good potential to enjoy a large number of activities and events.

3. Compute a cross-product score for each item and enter it in the column marked F X P. For example, if you did not go to the movies during the past 30 days (mark 0) but going to the movies is a very pleasant activity for you (mark 2), then the product score would be $0 \times 2 = 0$, and you would enter 0. If you have been watching television (Item 33) a great deal and you have therefore assigned it a frequency rating of 2, but you don't enjoy watching television and have, therefore, assigned it a pleasantness rating of 0, the product score would be $2 \times 0 = 0$. You are now ready to compute your *mean cross-product score* by adding the F X P scores of all 320 items and dividing this total by 320. The cross-product score is probably the most important score of this test because it is a measure of how much satisfaction and pleasure you derived from your activities during the past month. If the score is high, it means that you are deriving considerable pleasure and satisfaction from your activities, and the remainder of this chapter may not be particularly useful to you.

My mean frequency score is _____ .
My mean pleasantness score is _____ .
My mean cross-product score is _____ .

If your cross-product score is low, you can obtain one more useful bit of information by examining your score pattern. There are three possible patterns that can produce a low cross-product score.

Pattern 1—Low frequency/low pleasantness: You are not doing many of the activities on the list *and* you are not enjoying the activities that you do engage in.

Pattern 2—Low frequency/average or above-average pleasantness: You are not engaging in the kinds of activities that are potentially enjoyable for you.

Pattern 3—Average or above-average frequency/low pleasantness: You are doing many things but are not deriving much enjoyment from your activities.

Your score pattern can assist you later on in designing your self-change plan. If your scores have indicated Pattern 1, your first goal might be to increase the pleasure you obtain from your activities, and then, after you have accomplished this goal, aim to increase the number of pleasant activities you engage in. If your scores match Pattern 2, your goal can simply be to increase pleasant activities. If your scores have indicated Pattern 3, you might want to concentrate on increasing your enjoyment of the activities you are currently involved in.

Put a check mark next to the pattern that fits your PES scores.

Gathering Base-Line Data

The purpose of this section is the following:

1. To allow you to observe for yourself the degree to which your daily mood is related to your pleasant activities.
2. To assist you in setting a goal and in pinpointing the number of specific pleasant activities that need to be increased.

Developing and carrying out a self-change plan to increase the number of pleasant activities you do will take from four to six weeks, with time needed in between steps. For example, it requires two weeks of base-lining prior to setting a goal for increase. Your best bet is to read the remainder of this chapter to give you an overview. Then return to Step 1 and allow the time needed to complete each step before moving on to the next one.

You will self-observe on an individualized *Activity Schedule.* Your Activity Schedule will consist of 100 activities that are potentially pleasant for you. In order to construct an Activity Schedule, follow these steps:

STEP 1

Using the cross-product scores for individual items in Table 6–1, place a check mark in the *Check Items* column next to those activities with a cross-product score of 4. These are very pleasant activities, and you have been engaging in them during the past month. How many do you count?

Go back to the beginning of Table 6–1 and place a check mark in the same column next to activities with a cross product score of 2. How many check marks do you have now?

If your total is less than 100, continue to add activities from those with a *pleasantness* rating of 2 and a *frequency* rating of 0. These should have a cross-product score of 0. They are potentially pleasant activities, but you have not done them during the past 30 days. How many do you have now? If you are still short of 100, add some of the starred activities. These are the mood-related items. As you will recall, these activities have been found to be associated with mood for a fairly substantial proportion of the people who have taken our test. You should now have 100 activities, all of which are potentially pleasant for you.

STEP 2

This step will require more time and effort, and you should plan to reward yourself for completing it. Using the 100 items you have checked off in Step 1, write your own Activity Schedule on the form provided in the back of this book. This form will allow you to monitor your pleasant activities *and* your daily mood for 30 days. (Use Figure 6–1 as a model.) Because it is likely that you will want to monitor through more than a single month, make several copies of your Activity Schedule so that you will not have to write it again.

You are now ready to collect base-line data for your pleasant activities and to study their association with mood.

At the end of each day (select a regular time to do this, such as right after the 10 P.M. news), go down the Activity Schedule and place a check mark next to those activities or events that occurred during that day *and* which you experienced as pleasant. Because you are trying to monitor your *pleasant* activity level, do not check an activity if it was not at least somewhat pleasant. Compute your total pleasant-activity score by *adding* all the check marks for that day. Using the instructions given in Chapter 3, you should also rate your mood level for that day. Using the graph provided at the end of the book and the example shown in Figure 6–2 on page 95 as a model, plot your pleasant activity score and mood score for each day. Graphing will allow you to see the relationship between your activity level and your mood.

Self-observe your mood and your rate of engagement in pleasant activities during a period of two weeks. In doing the self-observing, it is helpful to keep an objective attitude. The goal is for you to learn something about yourself. You are not trying to prove anything to anybody, and you are not trying to change at this point. You are merely studying your own behavior and trying to see what relationships there may be between it and your depression.

After you have been self-observing for two weeks (you should definitely reward yourself for having mastered and completed this fairly difficult and new task), you are ready to begin using your compiled data.

The really important question you want to answer at this point is this: Is there an association (a correlation) between your rate of pleasant activities and your mood level? In the example shown in Figure 6–2, there clearly *is* a strong association; Mrs. B. feels much better on days when she engages in many pleasant activities than she does on days when she engages in very few of them. An easy way to determine whether there is an association between your pleasant activities and your mood is to add your activitity scores for your three most depressed days and then add your activities for your three best days. Is there a difference? As you can see from the example shown in Figure 6–1, Mrs. B's total pleasant-activity score for her three best days (Days 9, 25, 30) was 65 compared with 24 on her three worst days (Days 3, 6, 19).

To the extent that there is a positive association between your pleasant activities and your mood, it makes good sense to try to increase your pleasant activities if you want to feel better.

FIGURE 6–1
Activity Schedule Model

Activity	1	2	3	4	5	6	7	8	9	10	11	12	13	14	15	16	17	18	19	20	21	22	23	24	25	26	27	28	29	30
1. Reading stories, novels, or plays		✓	✓	✓			✓																							✓
2. Breathing clean air																		✓	✓							✓		✓	✓	
3. Saying something clearly		✓					✓			✓			✓					✓												
4. Having daydreams																						✓	✓	✓						
5. Writing stories, novels, plays, or poetry																								✓						
6. Being with animals	✓							✓	✓		✓	✓	✓	✓	✓	✓	✓	✓		✓										
7. Having a frank and open conversation						✓										✓	✓			✓	✓	✓	✓	✓	✓					✓
8. Working on my job																					✓									
9. Playing a musical instrument																														
10. Making food or crafts to sell or give away																											✓			
11. Watching wild animals													✓																	
12. Having an original idea																														
13. Talking about philosophy or religion							✓																✓		✓					
14. Listening to the radio		✓					✓				✓				✓	✓	✓	✓										✓		
15. Giving gifts										✓	✓																	✓		
...and so on through 100 items.																														
Total for Day	11	8	8	10	9	14	10	15	21	22	17	14	15	16	18	9	18	18	7	20	25	8	8	8	26	16	17	13	18	24
Mood Score	3	2	1	6	1	6	4	8	5	6	4	2	4	7	3	2	6	1	6	6	4	7	3	8	4	4	6	7	7	8

Day

FIGURE 6–2
Chart for Recording Daily Pleasant Activities and Mood Scores

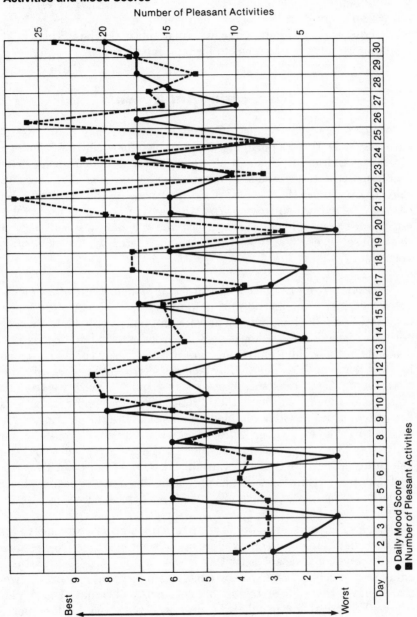

Number of Pleasant Activities

Daily Mood Score

Best

Worst

Day

● Daily Mood Score
■ Number of Pleasant Activities

There is other useful information that one can sometimes derive from the self-observation data. For example, you might discover that you always feel worse on Mondays (when you have to return to work) or on weekends (when you don't have a regular routine). These kinds of clues might be useful when it comes to formulating your plan.

Discovering Antecedents

Before developing a specific self-change plan, you may find it useful to spend a little time identifying the reasons for your low number of pleasant activities. In this section we will list and describe some *general* conditions that can produce a low number of pleasant activities. Typically, there is more than one reason. All (or none) of the examples we will cite may be applicable to you. You will have to decide on their relative importance to you. The idea is to assist you in choosing specific activities to increase. These "targets" will be needed later when you formulate your plan.

Pressure from activities that are not pleasant but must be done. There are many things most of us do that we may not experience as pleasant. Some of them may be down right unpleasant. Mothers seldom derive satisfaction from housework or from catering to the excessive demands of their children; taking care of a sick relative can be demanding; and many people do not enjoy some aspects of their work. However, if we neglect these responsibilities, we feel guilt, because we are letting other people down. But doing these things leaves us feeling resentful and frustrated. This is a fairly common problem. Part of the solution requires trying to achieve a better *balance* between unpleasant but necessary activities (Type A activities) and those activities a person would really like to do (Type B activities). Careful planning of one's time may be a useful step in organizing a self-change plan aimed at increasing pleasant activities in the face of strong pressure from Type A activities.

Lack of care in choosing activities with high pleasantness potential. In order to maintain our well-being, it is not necessary to engage in a large number of pleasant activities *if* we carefully choose activities we enjoy very much. Often we allow ourselves to drift into activities, which results in wasting time on things that we don't really enjoy. This might be especially critical for people who are very busy (e.g., those persons whose job demands leave very little time for Type B activities), and for older individuals and those with physical disabilities who may not be able to do some activities because the activities are too physically demanding. If this description fits you, give careful attention to selecting a small number of *really* enjoyable activities.

Many changes in a person's life situation have the effect of removing the necessity or the availability for potentially enjoyable, pleasant activities that have been extremely important to the person in the past. This is a common reason why many people have a low level of pleasant activities, and some examples may help to illustrate this point.

Example 1: Mary used to derive a great deal of satisfaction from planning and cooking meals and, in general, taking care of her family. Her children have left home, and her husband has died. Many of the potentially pleasant activities that played a very important part in her life are no longer needed.

Example 2: Bill, who enjoyed his work and the opportunities it provided him for social interaction, retired at age 65 and is now finding it difficult to fill his time.

Example 3: John recently graduated from college. He had enjoyed his school work (attending lectures, writing papers, reading books) because he was doing it well. However, such activities are not required for him to perform his work at his present job.

What these examples have in common is that each person's life situation has changed in such a way that many of the previous activities that had previously been so important to the person (housework, job, school, and so on) are no longer needed. A self-change plan for coping with this kind of situation should include a list of activities which will substitute for activities that have been lost because the person's environment no longer requires or needs them.

Anxiety and discomfort interfere with enjoyment. Your ability to derive pleasure from your activities may be reduced by the fact that you experience anxiety and tension in the situation.

Example 1: You are invited to a bridge party. You enjoy playing bridge, but you worry all the time about making mistakes.

Example 2: You are at a social gathering where you know many of the people. Nevertheless, you feel very uncomfortable and self-conscious.

If you see this type of pattern happening in your life and you realize that it is a major reason why you are not deriving much enjoyment from your activities, your plan should include learning how to relax (Chapter 5) and practicing relaxation in the situations in which you feel tense.

If tension interferes with your enjoyment of activities that would otherwise be pleasant for you, practicing relaxation techniques may be a useful component of your self-change plan. Tension may arise in the following three ways:

1. There is something about the potentially pleasant situation that makes you feel tense. For example, you enjoy playing bridge, but Mr. X is very critical of players who make mistakes, and you feel tense in his presence. Or, perhaps you enjoy being in small social gatherings, but after a while you start worrying about saying enough or saying the right things or wonder what other people are thinking about you.
2. Something has happened that has left you feeling upset, and, consequently, you derive little enjoyment from potentially pleasurable experiences. For example, you have just received some bad news, and you are unable to enjoy a visit with your daughter because you are still feeling upset. Or, you had an argument with your spouse that has left you feeling upset and you feel bad the rest of your day.
3. You are generally tense and tend to worry a lot, and this interferes with your ability to enjoy yourself.

If you have learned from Chapter 5 how to relax yourself, you have acquired a very useful skill for increasing your enjoyment in activities. If anxiety continues to be a problem for you, you should work on it in your self-change plan by making an active effort to relax yourself in situations in which you experience anxiety and tension.

In order to help you use what you have learned about the reasons for your having very few pleasant activities, try to summarize your conclusions.

The reasons I am not deriving any pleasure from my activities are the following:

☐ There is too much pressure from competing Type A activities.
☐ The activities I like to do are not needed by anyone.
☐ There is a poor match between what I do and what I really like to do.
☐ I feel too anxious and tense in situations I might otherwise enjoy.

Comments: _____

_____

_____

_____

In the line provided for your comments, try to be as specific as possible (e.g., I can't plan my activities because I never know when my husband is going to be home), and write out your conclusions. You will find it helpful in creating your plan.

Producing Your Plan

The goal of your plan is to accomplish a *modest* increase in your pleasant activity level from your base level. This may involve an increase in activities that you have done and found pleasant in the past, or it may involve engaging in activities that you have never done before but which you think might be pleasant.

It is very important that you set aside a specific time and place to develop (in writing) your plan. Be sure that you will not be interrupted or disturbed while you are doing it. The first step in planning is to set aside a specific time and place to first develop and then later examine and revise your plan.

We see planning as a very important component in your ability to implement any self-change procedure for the following reasons:

1. **Commitment**—By developing a plan for the coming week, you are making an explicit statement or agreement about how you would like to spend the next seven days. Making such a commitment helps you to make choices, to establish priorities, and to put things in perspective.
2. **Balance**—Having a plan allows you to examine the balance between activities that must be performed (Type A) and activities you really want to do (Type B). Achieving this kind of balance, as you will recall, is a very important goal in regard to combatting depression.
3. **Looking ahead**—Having a clear plan helps you to look ahead to see if there will be any problems that might interfere with carrying out the plan. For example, if you want to attend a show or a sports event on Wednesday afternoon, you may have to call a babysitter, arrange to have access to the family car or make other preparations for transportation, make a reservation, and so on. A very important part of planning is looking ahead and then making whatever arrangements need to be made in order to be able to follow through with the plan.
4. **Be prepared to resist demands**—Because you know what you want to do and when you want to do it, you will be in a much better position to resist demands on your time that might conflict with you plan.
5. **Control**—The more you are able to stick with you plan, the more you will achieve a *feeling of control*. This is a very important byproduct. If you feel that you are in control, you will be confident about giving active direction to your life. You will feel that you are not at the mercy of external forces, but rather you are in control of your own life. By controlling your time, you are able to control your life.

In making a practical plan, it is useful to distinguish between Type A and Type B activities. You are already familiar with this distinction. Let us try to clarify it further:

Type A Activities. These activities are neutral or unpleasant. They are activities in which we feel obligated to perform. Examples might be appointments with lawyers or dentists, cleaning the house, collecting debts, paying the bills, pulling weeds (unless you enjoy doing yard work), taking exams, applying for a job, being in a situation that makes you physically uncomfortable, and being in a social situation you don't want to be in. They are activities you experience as neutral or unpleasant but which you nevertheless feel need to be done; you would feel guilty if you did not do them.

Type B Activities. These are the activities we really like to do. They are the activities we wish to do whether anybody expects it of us or not. To say that Type A activities involve "work" whereas Type B activities involve recreation and fun is only partially correct, because some people enjoy their work-related activities. For example, students may look forward to reading a certain book that is relevant to a course they are taking, and musicians may look forward to playing their instruments. Thus, the distinction between Type A and Type B activities is set by how you feel about doing the activities. Is the activity one that you feel obligated to do even though you don't enjoy it (Type A), or is it something that you want to do because you expect to enjoy it (Type B)? Your activity schedule should consist *only* of Type B activities, and you should select from that list in making up your weekly plan. If you know of some Type B activities that are *not* on your schedule, add them to your list and cross out activities that you feel could easily be omitted. Keep the number of activities at 100.

Plan your time efficiently. There are some Type A activities (such as cleaning the house, writing a term paper, paying the bills, preparing the tax returns, or reading a book for an exam) that are done most efficiently if you allow a large block of time for them and do them at a time and place when you will not be interrupted or disturbed. On the other hand, there are some Type A activities (such as making a phone call, writing short letters, or paying bills) that can be squeezed into smaller blocks of time.

Look ahead. Be sure to include arrangements that have to be made in preparation for engaging in the planned activity. You may have to arrange for a babysitter, get tickets, get your cooking done early in the day, buy a fishing license, or purchase supplies for a camping trip.

You are now ready to make a self-change plan for yourself.

Setting a Specific Goal

Example: To obtain base-line data, Mike has been self-observing his daily mood and his pleasant activities for two weeks. After dividing his activity total for the two-week period (42) by the number of observation days (14), he was able to figure his average pleasant activities at three per day. Mike was struck by the fact that his daily totals vary quite a lot. On some days he didn't have any, and on one day he had seven.

For the graphing of his daily mood and pleasant-activity scores (for which he used the graph at the end of this book), Mike concluded that there was indeed an association between his mood and the level of his pleasant activities. He had felt more depressed on days when his pleasant-activity score was 0. On the basis of his base-lining, Mike set the following goals for the next two weeks:

1. He would not let his daily pleasant activities drop below four. Mike considers this very important.
2. Mike also committed himself to increasing his average daily pleasant activities to two for the following week. This meant that his total for the next two weeks would have to add up to 28.

Using *your* base-line data, set a goal for yourself:

My goal for the next week is to increase my average pleasant-activity score by ———. To do this I must bring my weekly total to ——— (multiply average by 7). I will also try to keep my pleasant-activity level from falling below ——— on any day (select a minimum you feel is realistic).

Be modest in setting your goal. Remember, it is more important for you to be successful than to try for a large increase and fail.

In order to carry out your plan, you will find it useful to *plan ahead* for each coming week by using a weekly plan (Figure 6–3).* Label each activity Type A or Type B by putting an A or a B after the activity. Are there too many As? If so, is it necessary that you do all of them next week? Are there some that you could transfer to the next week? What sort of balance do you have between the As and the Bs? How many hours each day are you spending on each? Will this plan for the coming week allow you to reach your goal for increase? Make changes in your weekly schedule as needed.

To help you evaluate this part of your plan, you should plan to check off with a red pen activities and events that you were not able to carry out as per your plan. Do this at the end of each day as part of your self-observing. This will tell you how realistic your goal is. Carefully review your weekly plan at the end of the week to help you evaluate how realistic it is and identify reasons why you were unable to stick with it. Don't worry about having a lot of red marks. It isn't easy to plan the week ahead, and unexpected things *will* happen. It takes practice. What *is* important is that, as you continue to do this throughout the weeks ahead, the number of red marks will be fewer. If you feel so inclined, you might actually count the number of red marks. They will become fewer as you get better at being able to plan your time.

*So that you can make additional copies for future use, a copy of the weekly plan form is included in the section titled *Extra Forms*, beginning on page 211.

FIGURE 6–3
Weekly Plan

Date:															
Time	8:00	9:00	10:00	11:00	12:00	1:00	2:00	3:00	4:00	5:00	6:00	7:00	8:00	9:00	10:00
Monday															
Tuesday															
Wednesday															
Thursday															
Friday															
Saturday															
Sunday															

As you are making your plan, you should be clear about the arrangements you will have to make to accomplish your plan. Another important part of your plan might be for you to make an active effort to be relaxed so that you can enjoy your planned activities.

Reward Yourself for Reaching Your Goals

It is useful to include in your plan a contract for rewarding yourself. What you are trying to do is not easy. In Chapter 2 you read about the importance of reinforcing yourself. The chances of your being able to carry out your plan successfully and to accomplish your goals will be far better if you plan to reward yourself.

We suggest that you construct a *reward menu:* a list of events and things you would like to have. Include only those rewards you are able to give to yourself. Do not include rewards that are dependent upon somebody else's behavior (e.g., your spouse's taking you out to dinner) unless you can be sure that you can count on the other person to keep his or her end of the agreement. Look at how you answered the Pleasant Events Schedule—this may help you in choosing a reward for yourself. Select events and objects that you would really enjoy doing or having.

Evaluation

You have two ways of deciding how well you are doing in following your plan. One is in terms of the self-observing data you will be gathering. Are you accomplishing your goal of achieving the kinds of increases you set out for yourself at the beginning of each week? Is your mood level getting better? The second way is in terms of using your weekly plan. Are you planning realistically? Are you making the arrangements that are necessary for you to stick with your schedule?

It is very important not to give up if things aren't perfect right away. Rome was not built in a day. It is very unlikely that you can immediately formulate a plan that is perfect, and you should not expect that it would be. The idea is to use the feedback that you will get from regularly evaluating your program. If something didn't work, try to make some changes that will improve your chances of success.

Getting Started

You now have a self-help plan designed to increase your pleasant activity level and thereby improve your mood. You have "diagnosed" yourself during the self-assessment part. You have used this information to define a specific increase in your pleasant activities, and you have made a specific plan for accomplishing this goal. Congratulations! You should have rewarded yourself with something special for having gotten this far!

Now you need to begin implementing the plan. The suggestions in this chapter may have made good sense to you and you would like to follow through, but perhaps you feel pessimistic. You may not be sure whether all this is worth the effort.

If you are finding it difficult to get started, it may be because of the following:

1. You have tried various treatments and self-help procedures in the past that did not work. Understandably, you feel pessimistic about this one.
2. You are feeling too depressed to make the effort this plan requires.
3. You are afraid to try this procedure because it might fail; and in that case, you might feel even more discouraged.

One or more of the above reasons may very well apply to you. There is no doubt that you are going to have to make a *real effort* to get started, that it is going to be difficult in the beginning, and that there are going to be failures and setbacks. But you can maximize the chances of being successful if you set modest goals and reward yourself for progress. Also, you should be prepared for setbacks and be willing to revise and improve your plan as you get more experience with it.

REVIEW

☐ I assessed my pleasant activities by completing the Pleasant Events Schedule in Table 6–1.
My mean frequency score was _____ .
My mean pleasantness score was _____ .
My mean cross-product score was _____ .

☐ I compared my mean cross-product score with the average scores for people my age and decided the following:
   ☐ A low number of pleasant activities is not one of my problems. I decided to start working on a different chapter.
   ☐ My level of pleasant activities is low in comparison to those of people my age.

☐ By examining my PES scores, I gained some additional information. Specifically, my scores suggest the following:
   ☐ I am not engaging in many pleasant activities, and I don't enjoy them when I do them (Pattern 1). An appropriate goal for me would be to focus on enhancing the pleasantness of my activities and then aim to increase the number of these activities.
   ☐ I am not engaging in activities that are potentially enjoyable for me (Pattern 2). An appropriate goal for me would be to increase my pleasant activities by doing more of the things I really enjoy doing.

☐ I am doing many things, but I'm not getting much pleasure or enjoyment from my activities (Pattern 3). An appropriate goal for me would be to deal with whatever is interfering with my enjoyment of these activities (e.g., tension, lack of care in choosing activities).

☐ I constructed an Activity Schedule for myself by identifying 100 activities (on the PES) with the highest cross-product scores and writing them on the Activity Schedule form in the back of the book.

☐ I rewarded myself by _____ for getting this far.

☐ Because I was still doing my daily mood ratings, I was ready to begin base-line observations.

☐ At the end of each day, for the next two weeks, I self-observed my mood and my pleasant activities and entered the scores on my Activity Schedule.

☐ During the base-line period, I also identified "reasons" (antecedents) for my low rate of pleasant activities. I gained some definite ideas and formulated them in concrete terms.

☐ I decided that feelings of tension and worrying seriously interfere with my being able to enjoy many of my activities. *I plan to take this into consideration in making my self-change plan.*

    ☐ Fortunately, I already know how to relax myself using the methods in Chapter 5 (or some other method).

    ☐ I decided that before proceeding with my pleasant activities self-change plan, I would need to learn how to reduce my feelings of tenseness in specific situations. I have referred to Chapter 5 and will return to this chapter when I am able to achieve a level of relaxation satisfactory to me.

☐ I have completed two weeks of base-line self-observations.

☐ At the end of the base-line period, I figured out my pleasant activities average, noting the lowest and the highest number.

☐ I also graphed my daily pleasant activities and mood scores. Inspecting my graph convinced me of the following:

    ☐ There is a definite association between what I do and my mood.

    ☐ There is no association between my activities and how I feel.

    ☐ I am not sure what the relationship is between what I do and how I feel.

☐ As soon as I was ready to make my self-change plan, the first thing I did was to set a specific goal for change. To help me achieve this goal, I did the following:

    ☐ I planned ahead for each coming week using the Weekly Plan shown in Figure 6–3.

    ☐ In planning ahead, I tried to achieve a balance between Type A and Type B activities.

    ☐ I made arrangements ahead of time so that I could do the activities I planned.

    ☐ I planned to make an active effort to feel relaxed in situations that tend to make me feel anxious.

☐ I wrote out my self-change plan so that I could more easily change it, or use it again in the future, if needed.

☐ I wrote a contract to reward myself for achieving my goal.

☐ I carried out my plan for increasing pleasant activities.

☐ I continued to self-observe my pleasant activities and daily mood during the implementation period.

☐ After one or two weeks, I evaluated my progress by doing the following:

    ☐ Determining whether I was accomplishing my goal for increasing pleasant activities. I did this by figuring my daily pleasant activities totals and comparing them with my goal.

    ☐ Determining whether my depression was diminishing. I did this by inspecting my daily mood scores.

    ☐ Seeing how realistic my planning ahead had been. I did this by seeing how many red marks there were in my weekly plan (Figure 6–3).

☐ On the basis of my evaluation, I decided the following:

    ☐ I was satisfied with my progress and would:

        ☐ Continue to use my self-change plan for another one or two weeks.

        ☐ Increase my goal.

    ☐ I was not satisfied with my progress and would:

        ☐ Change my goal.

        ☐ Change other aspects of my self-change plan.

7

Learning How to Be
Socially Skillful

You probably recall from Chapter 6 that many of the mood-related pleasant activities involve social interactions. These activities often have a critical effect on a person's state of depression. For many people, their depression level closely parallels the ups and downs of the quality and quantity of their personal relationships. Therefore, this chapter and Chapter 8 will be devoted specifically to social behavior.

We think about social skill as the ability to behave in ways that lead to positive reinforcement from other people, rather than punishment. In less psychological language, social skill is the ability to make people respond warmly and with interest to you, rather than ignoring you or getting upset with you.

There are a number of ways to be socially skillful. If you think about all the people you enjoy, you will probably find that they are different from each other. Some are quiet and gentle, some are funny and energetic, some are helpful and reliable, and so on. There is no *right* way to be or to get people to like and respect you; rather there are all kinds of different socially skillful behaviors. Therefore, this chapter *won't* tell you how to walk, talk, and smile—you won't have a script to learn. However, this chapter *will* suggest techniques you can use to change your behavior so that people will respond more positively to you. But you will have to use the suggestions in your own way and you will have to decide on many of the specific details to flesh out the techniques we suggest.

Because of studies conducted by psychologists, we know quite a bit about the social-skill problems of depressed people. We know, for example, that depressed people are less active than nondepressed people in many social situations. Depressed persons find it difficult to initiate contact with people they meet for the first time, and they tend to give and

107

receive fewer positive statements than other people do. In addition, depressed people are rated as less socially skillful than nondepressed people by people who observe them in social interactions. Depressed people are less comfortable in social situations, and they are especially sensitive to being ignored or rejected. Depressed people lack assertiveness; they don't stick up for themselves, and they don't say what they are thinking (whether it is good or bad).

These are just some of the social-skill problems that depressed people may have. Your particular problem may have been specifically mentioned, or you may have a slightly different problems from the ones mentioned here. If for any reason your interactions are not a source of pleasure for you, ask yourself a very important question: Does the problem exist because you never learned a better approach, or does the problem exist because you have stopped using skills you once had? This is important, because it is harder to learn new skills than it is to sharpen up skills you have but have let slide. This chapter will be devoted especially to helping people learn new skills. The next chapter is for people who are not presently using skills they once had.

Assertion

Jack had been looking forward to having dinner with his friend Adam. Jack and Adam are both in their early 60s and they work for the same company. Jack is looking forward to retirement, and he realizes that he has never gotten to know his friends well. When they no longer work together daily, he may never see them and he may not have anything in common to discuss with them. Jack hoped that he could get to know Adam better, but during dinner Jack missed several opportunities to be assertive and move the relationship forward. Here are some examples:

1. Jack's steak was tough and overcooked; he ate it without complaining and told the waitress everything was fine.
2. Jack had admired Adam's behavior during a conference that afternoon, but Jack was afraid to praise his friend.
3. Jack had hoped to get to know Adam better during dinner, but he didn't know how to talk about himself, so he ended up discussing the weather and local politics.
4. At one point, Jack disagreed with Adam's political views, but he was afraid to say so and pretended to agree.
5. When dinner was over, Jack wanted to suggest going into the bar to listen to a good singer who was performing, but he didn't. Instead, Jack went home and felt depressed, lonely, and discouraged.

Some people take a negative view of assertion. To them, being assertive means being loud, demanding, or obnoxious. Others view assertion more acceptingly, but still think mainly of its negative side. In this negative view, assertion consists mainly of things like expressing one's complaints in a frank manner, being insistent in demanding service, and refusing unreasonable requests from others.

Our view of assertion is much broader; we see it as the ability to express one's own thoughts and feelings openly, whatever they may be. Certainly that includes things like voicing complaints, but it also includes things like expressing growing feelings of warmth and affection, inviting other persons to share an activity, and letting other persons know about your hopes and fears. Being assertive means being willing to share oneself with other people rather than holding everything inside. Thus, assertion is a very important part of close, warm relationships. For most of us, such relationships are important, and we feel depressed when we don't have at least one or two of these positive, close relationships. Without being assertive in the way the term has been defined here, a person has very little chance of developing or maintaining the closeness and warmth that are so important for preventing or overcoming depression.

At a less philosophical and more practical level, it is important for people to learn to be assertive for other reasons as well. First, learning to be assertive helps you avoid or prevent aversive encounters with others; no one can take advantage of someone who is appropriately assertive. Second, those who are appropriately assertive are likely to get more positive responses from other people; they express more positive feelings, and they receive them in return. Assertive people say more, thus providing a chance for others to express their positive feelings in response. Finally, people who assert themselves feel better understood by other people. You have probably noticed that when you are depressed, you often feel isolated and cut off from other people; no one else seems to understand what you are feeling or wanting—and sometimes no one really seems to care. But people can't know how you feel and show their caring unless you take the first step by expressing your own thoughts and feelings.

How assertive are you? The questions listed in Table 7–1 are designed to help you decide whether you are assertive and how comfortable you are with assertion. They will also help you pinpoint situations where assertive behavior is appropriate. Review the list of questions twice: the first time, rate each item on how often the situation has occurred in the past month; the second time, rate how comfortable you were (or, if the situation did not occur, how comfortable you *would* be if it were to happen). There are no right or wrong answers to these questions; their purpose is to provide you with information about yourself. Please read over the instructions at the start of the questionnaire, then work quickly, making two ratings for every item.

TABLE 7–1
Assertion Questionnaire

Rating frequency of assertion

Indicate how often each of these events occurred by marking Column A, using the following scale:

    1 . . .   This has *not* happened in the past 30 days.
    2 . . .   This has happened *a few times* (1 to 6 times) in the past 30 days.
    3 . . .   This has happened *often* (7 times or more) in the past 30 days.

Rating how you feel about assertion

Indicate how you feel about each of these events by marking Column B, using the following scale:

    1 . . .   I felt *very uncomfortable or upset* when this happened.
    2 . . .   I felt *somewhat uncomfortable or upset* when this happened.
    3 . . .   I felt *neutral* when this happened (neither comfortable nor uncomfortable; neither good nor upset).
    4 . . .   I felt *fairly comfortable or good* when this happened.
    5 . . .   I felt *very comfortable or good* when this happened.

Important: If an event has not happened during the past month, than rate it according to how you *think you would feel if it happened*. If an event happened more than once in the past month, rate roughly how you felt about it *on the average*.

                                                              A   *B*

1. Turning down a person's request to borrow my car
2. Asking a favor of someone
3. Resisting sales pressure
4. Admitting fear and requesting consideration
5. Telling a person I am intimately involved with that he/she has said or done something that bothers me
6. Admitting ignorance in an area being discussed
7. Turning down a friend's request to borrow money
8. Turning off a talkative friend
9. Asking for constructive criticism
10. Asking for clarification when I am confused about what someone has said
11. Asking whether I have offended someone
12. Telling a person of the opposite sex that I like him/her
13. Telling a person of the same sex that I like him/her
14. Requesting expected service when it hasn't been offered (e.g., in a restaurant)
15. Discussing openly with a person his/her criticism of my behavior
16. Returning defective items (e.g., at a store or restaurant)
17. Expressing an opinion that differs from that of a person I am talking with
18. Resisting sexual overtures when I am not interested

Assertion Questionnaire *(cont.)*

	A	B

19. Telling someone how I feel if he/she has done something that is unfair to me
20. Turning down a social invitation from someone I don't particularly like
21. Resisting pressure to drink
22. Resisting an unfair demand from a person who is important to me
23. Requesting the return of borrowed items
24. Telling a friend or co-worker when he/she says or does something that bothers me
25. Asking a person who is annoying me in a public situation to stop (e.g, smoking on a bus)
26. Criticizing a friend
27. Criticizing my spouse
28. Asking someone for help or advice
29. Expressing my love to someone
30. Asking to borrow something
31. Giving my opinion when a group is discussing an important matter
32. Taking a definite stand on a controversial issue
33. When two friends are arguing, supporting the one I agree with
34. Expressing my opinion to someone I don't know very well
35. Interrupting someone to ask him/her to repeat something I didn't hear clearly
36. Contradicting someone when I think I might hurt him/her by doing so
37. Telling someone that he/she has disappointed me or let me down
38. Asking someone to leave me alone
39. Telling a friend or co-worker that he/she has done a good job
40. Telling someone he/she has made a good point in a discussion
41. Telling someone I have enjoyed talking with him/her
42. Complimenting someone on his/her skill or creativity

TABLE 7–2

Assertion Scores: Normal Range	
Frequency	61–81
Comfort	102–137

In order to score the questionnaire, add up all the frequency ratings and then add up all the comfort ratings. Compare your scores to the scores shown in Table 7–2. If you find that either of your scores is lower than the score at the lower end of the range in Table 7–2, you may want to concentrate on becoming more assertive. The next section of this chapter is written to help you with that goal. If your scores are higher than the averages shown in the table, you are most likely appropriately assertive. In this case, you may want to skip ahead to page 119 in this chapter.

Let's go through a few examples to make sure that the procedure you must follow to interpret the questionnaire is clear. Let's assume that Jack, the man described at the beginning of this section, answered these questions. After he added up his scores, he had a total of 54 for frequency and a total of 88 for comfort. These scores are clearly below the ranges provided in Table 7–2, so Jack should conclude that he is less often assertive than the average person and less comfortable than average about being assertive. Next, let's assume that Jack answered the questions again after working on becoming more assertive. This time Jack's frequency score was 67 and his comfort score was 100. This means that Jack is now as assertive as often as the average person, but he is still a little uncomfortable about it. Finally, let's assume that Jack keeps working at being assertive and is quite successful. This time his scores are 77 for frequency and 142 for comfort. This would mean that Jack is assertive as often as the average person, but he is clearly on the upper end of the distribution—and he is more comfortable about being assertive than the average person.

Learning How to Be Assertive

Now that you are familiar with the concept of assertion, it is time to begin incorporating assertiveness directly into your own life. At this point, you may feel convinced that you would like to be more assertive, but you are baffled about how to begin. The rest of this section will describe a method for you to use to learn to be more assertive in your daily life.

The next step is to develop a Personal Problem List. This is a list of from five to ten situations that meet all of the following criteria:

1. You are currently handling the situation in a nonassertive manner.
2. The situation occurs regularly in your life (at *least* once a month).
3. The situation is troubling to you.
4. The situation strikes a good balance between being too specific ("My mother complaining about the pot roast I cooked last night") and too general ("Anyone complaining to me about anything"). A good balance might be: "My family complaining to me about my behavior." If the item is too specific, it may never occur again, and if it is too general, it may be difficult to find a way of dealing with it that will fit all the possible situations.
5. The different situations on the list should be reasonably different from each other; if the situations are too similar, merge the items.
6. The different situations should cover a diverse number of areas (home, school, work, shopping, dining out, and so on), and types of behavior

(resisting pressure, expressing warmth, making requests, handling disagreements, and so on), unless you have difficulty in only one area.

As you write your list, be sure to consider items from the assessment
you just completed. The following sample list may help as you prepare
your own.

Personal Problem List

1. Telling Jack that I am bothered by something he did.
2. Initiating plans to get together with my friends, especially with new
   friends.
3. Expressing my preference to my husband about how we spend our free
   time together.
4. Asking my supervisor at work for more feedback about how I am doing.
5. Calling to cancel an appointment.
6. Apologizing to my family when I let them down.
7. Walking out of a store without buying things when a salesperson gets
   pushy.
8. Telling the neighbors about my complaints (about their noise, letting
   dogs run loose, and so on).
9. Telling my husband I need more time with him.
10. Introducing myself to new people at parties.

Keeping Track of Your Assertion

After you have completed your list, turn to the Self-Monitoring of
Assertion Form in Figure 7–1. On this form, write in the ten situations
on your Personal Problem List; add more lines if you have more than ten
items. Make a habit of keeping track of your assertiveness *every day* in
all ten of the situations. To do this, follow these instructions: Each day, fill
out a copy of the personalized form. For each situation, rate how
comfortable you were (from 0 to 10) and how skillful you were in
asserting yourself (from 0 to 10) *each time a situation occurred*. Be sure
to rate every occasion on which the situation occurred; on some days, that
may be more than once. A 0 rating indicates a totally unsatisfactory
performance (you were completely uncomfortable, or you were completely nonassertive). You would also rate 0 if you *avoided* the situation
when it arose. A rating of 10 indicates near perfection in performance
(you were completely relaxed and comfortable, or you were extremely
skillful in your assertive behavior). Most ratings, of course, will fall
between these two extremes and should reflect *your own evaluation* of
your comfort and assertion in particular situations.

The reason we want you to keep track of your behavior is so that you
can see how your behavior changes during a period of time as you use the

FIGURE 7–1
Self-Monitoring of Assertion Form

Situation	Comfort	Skill in Asserting Myself
1.		
2.		
3.		
4.		
5.		
6.		
7.		
8.		
9.		
10.		

suggested techniques.* Be sure to keep all of your rating forms so that you can look back later and see your progress. Also, after each week it is a good idea to figure out your average comfort and skill ratings for each situation. Your day-to-day ratings will probably vary quite a bit, but the weekly averages should show fairly steady progress.

Practicing Assertive Imagery

After a week of self-monitoring, you will be ready to begin practicing assertion in your own imagination. This procedure, which will be explained in detail, will give you maximum flexibility because you can practice as often as you want, wherever you want. In the privacy of your own mind, you can try out numerous responses and refine your own personal style without making your mistakes out loud. You can practice handling situations that vary in small but important ways (for instance, whether you are asking a request of a male or a female) because you create the situation in your head. In this way, you will be entirely in

*So that you can make additional copies for use in subsequent weeks, the Self-Monitoring of Assertion Form is included in the section titled *Extra Forms*, beginning on page 211.

control and will be prepared to try out your new skill in reality, with other people. Anticipating situations in this way makes it more likely that you will be able to handle situations when they occur.

Begin your sessions by focusing on one or two of the ten situations on your personalized list. There are three basic strategies for choosing where to start. You can pick the two situations that seem easiest to you, so that you are assured of some success at the start. Or, you can pick the two situations that are more likely to happen soon so that you will be prepared for them. Or, you can pick any two situations at random and just get started. Any of these strategies will work; use the one that appeals to you the most.

For the first few sessions you should practice at least fifteen minutes every day, and you should conduct most of your practice sessions in a place where you can concentrate well and will not be interrupted—for example, in your bedroom or lying down on the living-room couch. Later on, you can be more flexible about where, when, and how often you can practice, but at the start you should take extra care to create a good practice environment for yourself.

Creating Vivid Images

In each session, be sure to follow these steps. First, select one of your situations and imagine a concrete example of that situation. Close your eyes and imagine the scene; try to vividly imagine where the situation occurs, who is there, and where you are in the scene. Get a real picture of the scene in your imagination, as if you could see a photograph of it, and then start the action and turn the photograph into a movie. In the movie, imagine what each person is saying and doing, and picture the events leading up to the moment when you will want to assert yourself. Then imagine, as clearly as you can, your own behavior; imagine yourself saying something that you would feel very good about in that situation. What you say should be assertive, not passive or aggressive. It should please you; you should feel that you would be satisfied with yourself if you actually handled the situation that way. What you say doesn't have to be witty, charming, earth shattering, or the ultimate assertive act. It should simply be a way to handle the situation that pleases you. Then imagine what would happen after you demonstrated your assertiveness; what would the other people say and do? Usually, it is a good idea to imagine the positive effects of your behavior; in fact, most assertion *will* be received well. However, it won't *always* be, and you should occasionally imagine that other people do not react to your assertiveness in a positive way. In that case, remember that the *goal is to handle the situation as well as you can*, not to manipulate, control, or predict the actions of other people.

After completely running through a scene once, go back and do the same scene again, except change some of the details. Change one of the people, or change what is said that leads up to your assertion, or change the content of your assertive behavior slightly. Continue this sequence several times; each time follow the complete sequence, but change it in some way from the last time through. The sequence should always contain the following:

A *vivid image* of the scene—as if it were a *photograph* which turns into

A *movie* that shows what leads up to your

Assertive statement, which should be satisfying to you and which creates a

Response, usually positive, from the other people in the scene.

The following are examples of such an imagery sequence; obviously, you will have to supply the relevant visual images in your own mind. In the following example, the situation on the personalized monitoring list was "Expressing my preference to my husband about how we should spend our free time together."

FIRST SEQUENCE

Photograph: You are with your husband; you have both arrived home from work on Friday afternoon and are sitting in the living room playing with the dogs and having a drink. You are a little tired and would like to go out to dinner and then go for a walk by the river.

Movie: The dogs are playing a little bit, but are not too distracting. Your husband sits up, scratching one dog's head. He looks across the room and says, "I've been thinking, and I'm not really sure what we should do tonight. There's a good movie on, but maybe we should play racquetball and get some exercise."

You start to feel a little anxious, but the dog looks up at you and licks your hand, so you decide to be brave in your reply.

Assertion: "Both of those would be all right with me, but I would *really* like to do something else. I'd like it if we could go out for dinner and then take a walk by the river. It's a lovely evening, and I think it would be relaxing for us both to be outside for a while after working inside all day."

Response: Your husband looks a little reluctant, but thoughtfully replies, "I guess that sounds OK to me. Maybe we could play racquetball tomorrow morning when we're rested. How about if we go to the Excelsior for dinner? Does that sound good?"

SECOND SEQUENCE:

Photograph: Same scene as before, except that it is winter instead of summer. It is dark outside, and there is a fire burning in the fireplace. You would like to spend the evening at home, talking and planning your weekend trip to the coast.

Movie: You chat for a while about the day; you feel relaxed. You get up and poke the fire, then throw on another log. Turning away from the fire, your husband says, "Do you think we should call some friends and invite them over?" You consider your reply.

Assertion: "That sounds like we would be up pretty late, and we wanted to get an early start tomorrow. Maybe we should stay home and plan which road to take to the coast tomorrow. Then we could get ready, get to bed early, and get started early in the morning."

Response: "Sounds like a good idea to me. I'm kind of tired tonight, anyway."

Creating Your Own Examples for Your Personalized Problem List

Now try out a few examples using one of your own situations; then write out the essential elements, as in the examples given here. You can be brief and just capture the major images and words. Check to make sure that all four components are there. Especially check to make sure that you are satisfied with your assertion. If you feel you need help at this stage, try asking a friend or relative to review the scenes with you and make helpful suggestions.

Once you are satisfied with your ability to produce appropriate scenes, set up a schedule for this week's practice. Try to schedule your practice at a regular time and place. Remember, you should practice at least fifteen minutes every day, using two of the situations on your personalized list. Be sure to continue monitoring your behavior in all ten of the situations every time they occur.

Transferring from Imagery to Real Life

After a week of imagery practice, you should be ready to begin trying out your skills in the real world. Remember that at first it will be a little awkward, but every time you try it, assertion will feel a little more natural. At first, you should try to anticipate the situations for trying out your skills, rather than waiting and hoping that a good chance will come along. Try to plan situations that are most likely to be successful. For example, if making a request is one of the items on your list, try to ask a kind, generous person for help rather than choosing someone who is usually grouchy. Or, if offering a compliment is an item on your list, try to do it casually and privately, rather than putting someone else in an awkward position. Rehearse the real-life situation as explicitly as you can *before* you try it. Be sure to rate the situations you plan, along with the naturally occurring ones, on your self-monitoring forms.

Evaluating Your Progress

After ten days of practicing assertions, you should evaluate your progress. Go back over the rating forms and your average scores. Are they improving? If you have successfully practiced the imagery and used it in a real-life situation, you are well on the way to becoming an appropriately assertive person. All that remains is to repeat exactly the same sequence of steps using the other items on your personalized list. Choose about two items at a time to work on, first in imagery and then in real life. You can begin to make your schedule more flexible. Try the imagery while waiting for service, riding the bus, or taking a coffee break. Just be sure to continue doing it *regularly*—at least ten minutes every day. You can also begin to be more flexible about the real-life use of the technique. You might start taking advantage of naturally occurring situations, as well as setting up optimal situations for yourself. You now have the basic tools you need to improve your skill at being assertive. Hold on to the basic tool, but also begin to explore its possibilities while you improve.

If you are not making progress yet, you should try to understand why this is so and where you should make some changes. Here are some possibilities:

1. You may have a long history of being very nonassertive. If this is the case, you probably need more time using this technique; stick with it for another few weeks.
2. You may not be practicing as often as you need, or you may be taking "shortcuts" with the techniques. Make sure that you are practicing regularly, that you are creating good, vivid images, and that you are taking time to go through the whole scene carefully.
3. You may be setting very high standards for yourself and not admitting progress in your ratings if your images or behavior are not perfect. Use the whole scale from 0 to 10; don't wait until you can give yourself a perfect 10 before you upgrade your ratings.

4. If you have tried these suggestions and are still not making progress, this may not be the technique for you. Not everyone improves using the same method, and you may respond beautifully to another method. There are a number of books on the market designed to help people increase their assertive behavior. Probably the best one is *Your Perfect Right* by Alberti and Emmons.* Other books you might find helpful are listed in the back of this book. Or you might want to seek additional help from a counselor.

How Do You Appear to Others?

Gloria is a depressed, 38-year-old woman. Watching Gloria while she sits with a group of acquaintances is very informative. The group is sitting in a circle, but Gloria's chair is three feet further back than the chairs of the other people. The diagram below shows the seating arrangement. Gloria is sitting in chair 1; she could pull her chair forward to become a part of the group, but she has not chosen to do that. Gloria is looking down at the floor while she sits. Her hands are in her lap, her right hand fidgeting with a ring on her left hand. When she looks up occasionally, her face appears nervous and unhappy; she never smiles. Other people in the group ask her questions from time to time; Gloria's answers are halting, and there are long pauses between words. Sometimes she doesn't answer at all, so the conversation eventually goes on without her. When Gloria does talk, she usually complains about how bad she feels; she says nothing positive to anyone in the group.

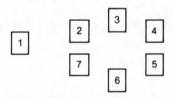

Obviously, Gloria's behavior is that of a depressed person. But why is it happening—is she acting this way because she is depressed, or are her feelings of depression perhaps caused by her social withdrawal? No one can say for sure, but Gloria's unpleasant social behavior may be contributing to her depression. Certainly she is creating a situation that ensures that she stays depressed. The others in the circle are bothered by her unfriendliness, and they gradually say less and less to her. Next time the group meets, Gloria may not be included at all. Then she will feel even more lonely and depressed, and she will be even less pleasant to be around. This sets up a vicious circle, which may become very difficult for Gloria to break.

*R. E. Alberti, and M. Emmons, *Your Perfect Right*, 2nd ed. (San Luis Obispo, Calif.: Impact, 1974).

It is striking to observe a really depressed person like Gloria; the depression often shows clearly without the person's ever saying that he or she feels depressed. Try observing someone you know who is depressed. Like Gloria, that person (let's assume it's a female friend) is likely to smile very little, to look at the floor or her lap instead of at you, and to sit slouched over rather than looking interested and alert. She may also speak very slowly or very softly so that it is hard to hear what she is saying. It is also likely that she will not use illustrative hand gestures while speaking; instead, she may use nervous gestures like playing with a paper clip or rubbing her hand on her leg. This may be distracting or irritating to you. Your friend may also neglect to show much interest in what you say and, thus, make you feel like she would rather have you leave her alone. All these things combine to create in you a strong feeling that your friend is unhappy, even though you may not know why she is unhappy. You will probably feel uncomfortable while you are with her, and you may have a vague feeling of guilt because you somehow feel responsible about doing something for her. If this has happened several times, you may find yourself avoiding your friend in the future. Now, the real question is: Do *you* affect other people in this way when *you* are depressed? It is possible that you do. However, it will be difficult for you to judge this for yourself. Look over the following list and check off, as honestly as you can, all the behaviors that seem to be true of you. Discuss this information with a close, trusted friend if you possibly can; the two of you should then be able to make a decision together about whether this is a problem area for you.

- [ ] Not smiling; unpleasant facial expression
- [ ] Failing to make eye contact
- [ ] Not joining in conversations
- [ ] Whining
- [ ] Complaining or brooding out loud about problems
- [ ] Slumping over while sitting or standing
- [ ] Poor grooming
- [ ] Nervous gestures
- [ ] Not asking questions or otherwise showing interest in what other persons are saying
- [ ] Speaking too softly; making it difficult for others to hear you
- [ ] Slow, halting speech
- [ ] Telling your troubles to everyone
- [ ] Crying often in public
- [ ] Not responding to questions
- [ ] Criticizing others
- [ ] Ignoring others
- [ ] Other problem: _____

These problems illustrate the kinds of things that influence the impact we have on others; you may be able to add other examples to the list. If you feel you are having a negative impact on others, the important thing for you to do is to pinpoint a few areas that you can change and which are most likely to lead to success. You can do that by using our list or by coming up with items on your own.

How do you go about changing these things? Recall the basic way we have set up changes throughout this book. First, set up specific goals for yourself that proceed in small, gradual steps. Second, keep track of your behavior in order to make sure you are actually improving. Third, reward yourself for progress; reward small gains rather than insisting on immediate perfection.

To make these steps concrete, let's use the first item, *Not smiling*, as an illustration. Here is a sample set of small, gradual steps toward improvement. For an illustration, let's use Gloria's list:

1. Smile at myself in the mirror at least three times a day.
2. Smile at my co-workers at least twice a day.
3. Smile at my co-workers at least five times a day.
4. Smile at my co-workers at least once each time I speak to one of them.
5. Smile at friends outside of work at least once a day.
6. Smile at friends outside of work at least once each time I speak to them.

Gloria set her list up this way because she felt most awkward about smiling with friends, and she was most tempted to cry and talk about her problems with her friends. It was easier for her to start with co-workers. She gave herself a week to accomplish each step. By the end of the week, she expected herself to meet or exceed her goal. If she did, she rewarded herself with either new clothes or a good lunch at a restaurant on Saturday; then she started the next step on Sunday. She progressed well at most steps; however, Step 4 took her two weeks to accomplish and Step 6 also took her two weeks. Thus, the whole process of change took eight weeks—or about two months. That may seem like slow progress, but because Gloria kept at it steadily and in discrete steps, she could see her improvement every week in the records she was keeping.

Set up similar steps for yourself for any of the items that seem to be important for you. Try to keep in mind the overall goal: You want to stop driving people away with your negative behavior. You don't have to be a phony, or give up honest emotions, or act like a cheerful circus clown. You simply want to be a reasonably pleasant person rather than someone to avoid. If possible, have a good friend help you keep track of how you are doing.

Moving to a New
Social Environment

James moved to San Francisco in January, and by March he was miserable. His job was OK; his apartment was OK; his family whom he had left behind loved him and missed him; his cat was always waiting for him when he came home; and he read a lot of good books. He knew San Francisco had a symphony, an opera, beautiful parks, museums, restaurants, nightclubs, and theaters—but he didn't know where they were, how to get around in the city, how to enjoy doing things by himself, or where to meet people he might enjoy. So he stayed home with his cat, read books, and got depressed living in one of the most interesting cities in the world.

This kind of depression can occur when people move, when they change jobs or schools, when a company is reorganized, or when almost any situation involving change occurs. The skill that James lacks is a simple one—he doesn't know how to gather and act on information about social activities. The discussion about this problem serves as a bridge between this chapter, which emphasizes learning new skills, and the next chapter, which emphasizes skills that are available but are not being used. Learning to collect information in a new environment doesn't fit exactly into either category, but we can offer a few brief hints here about getting to know a new environment; the next chapter should also be useful if this is one of your problems.

In your efforts to adapt to living in any new territory, you should ask yourself the following questions: Where are the people? Where are the activities? What parts of town should be avoided? How formal or informal are people here? What is available to someone on a tight budget? What activities are available to older adults? What transportation is available? What child care is available for single parents? These, and a host of similar questions, weigh heavily on a new arrival and interfere with socializing. Luckily, these questions are not difficult to answer, as long as you display some initiative.

The following list contains some suggestions for things you can do. Many of these ideas are also found in *First Person Singular*, by Stephen M. Johnson.* You may also want to read Dr. Johnson's book for further ideas.

---

*S. M. Johnson, *First Person Singular: Living the Good Life Alone* (Philadelphia: Lippincott, 1977).

1. Subscribe to the local paper and read the activities and entertainment section faithfully. You can also find out about events sponsored by the community's religious groups that fit your beliefs.
2. Ask the local Chamber of Commerce for information. It can usually supply a good deal of information about groups and activities in the area.
3. Go out a lot and be prepared to *make mistakes*. There's no teacher like experience. You may waste a few evenings or weekends, but you'll learn a lot and maybe you'll find someone else who is exploring, also.
4. Call someone—anyone you know at work, a neighbor, or a classmate. Don't ask for friendship—just explain your situation and ask for information. You may get both information *and* friendship.
5. Spend several weekends exploring. Get a map of town and a good pair of shoes, and plan a number of exploring trips. Walk all over a section of town; scout out the shops, restaurants, theaters, and other areas where people might congregate. Make a list of what you find; then when you're looking for a good restaurant, you will have a good selection of places to try.
6. Join a group that does interesting things in the area; for example, a hiking club, a theater group, a sports club, a senior center, or whatever sounds attractive to you. At this stage, it is probably better to avoid joining groups that meet in the same place every week to do the same thing; that can come later. Right now, you want to get a variety of experiences. If you know you would really enjoy a group that meets regularly for one purpose, go ahead and join it. But don't limit yourself by stopping there.

If you've tried all these suggestions and you're still having trouble becoming sociable, you need to examine more closely the reasons why. It may be that just learning about social environments is not enough for you. You may need a more systematic approach to increasing your social activities. The next chapter is designed to help you do that.

SUMMARY

This chapter has covered three different kinds of problems that depressed people often experience; lack of assertiveness, having a negative impact on other people because of personal style, and failure to learn about social environments. For each problem area, a strategy was suggested for improvement. If you selected this chapter as one of your areas of concentration, you should now have a clearer idea of what your own specific problems with people are and what you can do about them. You should have a plan of action and you should be keeping records of your behavior. You will soon be seeing changes in your behavior as you implement you plan. And, as always, you can use your daily records of your mood to see whether changing you social behavior is helping you become less depressed.

REVIEW

☐ I understand what assertion is and why it is important.

☐ I have filled out the Assertion Questionnaire in Table 7–1 and evaluated my scores.

☐ If either of my scores on assertion was low, I am working on becoming more assertive and/or comfortable about assertion. To accomplish this goal, I have done the following:

    ☐ Made a Personal Problem List

    ☐ Assessed my comfort and assertive skill in each of the situations on my list evey day

    ☐ Practiced, in imagery, behaving assertively in situations on my list.

    ☐ Begun trying out my assertiveness in real-life situations.

    ☐ Evaluated my progress at least once.

☐ I have gone over the checklist of negative behaviors. If I decided that one or more of these are typical of me, I have done the following:

    ☐ Set up a change plan, using small steps, self-monitoring, and rewards for small gains.

    ☐ Worked on my plan for at least two weeks.

    ☐ Evaluated my progress at least once.

☐ I have decided whether the section on learning about new social environments is applicable to my situation. If it is, I have done the following:

    ☐ Tried out at least one of the techniques suggested.

    ☐ Evaluated my progress at least once.

    ☐ Decided whether to go on to the next chapter to use a more systematic approach to increasing my social activities.

Using Your Social Skills

Janet is a lonely, depressed person. She hadn't always been lonely. In fact, until last year no one would have suspected that she could be so lonely. Janet had always been friendly and easy to get to know; she had a warm smile and a relaxed, comfortable personal style. She had been able to assert herself, and she was always able to make new friends. So why is Janet lonely now?

There are a number of reasons. A year ago, Janet gave birth to her first child, which resulted in her voluntarily giving up a number of activities she had shared with friends. She told herself this was only temporary, but somehow she didn't keep track of the time. Six months later, she realized that "temporary" was becoming "permanent." She and her husband no longer enjoyed the people or activities they once had, and they had stopped inviting couples over to their house to visit. They had turned down so many invitations right after the baby was born that their friends were no longer inviting them out. Janet still hadn't planned a new daily schedule for herself, so there was no regular time of day when she could count on making arrangements to go out with friends.

In short, Janet is in a rut. She has set up a life schedule that leaves no room for friends, and she isn't doing anything to change that situation. She becomes lonelier and more depressed every day. The more depressed she gets, the more helpless and tired she feels. She enjoys her family less, has less interest in life, and has less to talk about when she does see friends. Janet still has the potential to make friends and enjoy social interaction, but she isn't using her abilities at all.

This story about Janet illustrates a common problem among depressed people. Janet knows how to be socially skillful, but she isn't using what she knows. She doesn't need to learn new skills; she mainly needs to arrange her life differently so that she can use the skills she already has.

Another similar problem is often experienced by socially anxious people. They have the skills, but being in social situations in general, or in certain social situations in particular, makes them feel fearful or uncomfortable. For these people, as for Janet in the previous illustration, knowing *what* to do isn't enough. They need help in overcoming whatever prevents them from using what they know. The purpose of this chapter is to provide such help.

Evaluating Yourself

After taking the following test, you will be able to evaluate your level of social participation. Table 8–1 lists activities that are usually shared with other people—review this list twice. The first time, you should rate each activity on how often it has occurred in the past month; the second time, you should rate how comfortable you felt during the activity (or, if the activity did not occur, how comfortable you *would* be if it were to occur). There are no right or wrong answers to these questions; their purpose is to provide you with information about yourself. Please work quickly and rate *every* activity. After you have rated each item on frequency and comfort, you can go on to the next section.

To score your activities, first add the ratings on comfort for each of the items. This is your *comfort score* (it can also be thought of as your social-anxiety score). Compare your score to those listed in Table 8–2, which shows high and low scores based on normative data for nondepressed adults. If your score is lower than the low score shown, then you should read Chapter 5, *Relaxation*, which presents a detailed plan for learning how to relax and how to overcome anxiety by using relaxation in your everyday life.

Next, add the frequency ratings for each of the items; this is your *frequency score*. Compare your score to those shown in Table 8–2. If your score on social participation is lower than the score shown, you will probably want to plan ways to become more active with other people. The remainder of this chapter is designed to help you with that goal.

If your comfort score is low and your frequency score is high, you will just need to work with Chapter 5. If your comfort score is high but your frequency score is low, you will just need to work with this chapter. If both scores are low, decide which area to work on first, but plan to work on both. If both scores are high, pat yourself on the back and move on to another problem area.

TABLE 8–1
Social Activities Questionnaire

Rating how often social activities occur

Indicate how often you did each of the following activities by marking Column A, using the following scale:

1. . . . . . . This has *not* happened in the past 30 days.
2. . . . . . . This has happened *a few times* (1 to 6 times) in the past 30 days.
3. . . . . . . This has happened *often* (7 times or more) in the past 30 days.

Rating how you feel about each social activity

Indicate how you feel about each of the following activities by marking Column B, using the following scale:

1. . . . . . . I felt *very uncomfortable or upset* when this happened.
2. . . . . . . I felt *somewhat uncomfortable or upset* when this happened.
3. . . . . . . I felt *neutral* when this happened (neither comfortable nor uncomfortable; neither good nor upset).
4. . . . . . . I felt *fairly comfortable or good* when this happened.
5. . . . . . . I felt *very comfortable or good* when this happened.

Important: If an event has *not* happened to you during the past month, then rate according to how you think you would feel if it happened. If an event happened more than once in the past month, rate roughly how you felt about it *on the average.*

                                                                      A   B

1. Talking with a friend
2. Going on a recreational outing (boating, camping, hiking, etc.)
3. Being in a class, discussion group, or encounter group
4. Going on my first date with someone
5. Receiving a telephone call from a friend
6. Initiating a conversation with a stranger
7. Talking with my parent(s)
8. Being asked for my help or advice
9. Going to an office party
10. Talking with my child(ren) or grandchild(ren)
11. Visiting friends
12. Doing volunteer work or working on a community service project
13. Accepting a date or social invitation
14. Dancing
15. Being the first to say "hello" when I see someone I know
16. Having lunch or a coffee break with friends
17. Going to a bar or tavern
18. Introducing myself to someone
19. Talking with a stranger of the same sex
20. Introducing people I think would like each other
21. Going to a sports event (football, track meet, etc.)
22. Singing or playing a musical instrument in a group
23. Talking with my husband or wife

Social Activities Questionnaire *(cont.)*

	A	B

24. Going on a date
25. Being introduced to someone
26. Going to a church function
27. Playing cards or board games (checkers, Monopoly, etc.)
28. Going to a party
29. Inviting a friend or acquaintance to join me for some social activity
30. Walking up and joining a group of people
31. Going to a service, civic, special interest, or social club meeting
32. Going someplace where I know I must be sociable
33. Talking with someone on the job or in class
34. Talking with a stranger of the opposite sex
35. Joining a friend or friends for a social activity
36. Giving a party or get-together
37. Calling a friend on the telephone
38. Having sexual relations
39. Going to a formal social affair
40. Having friends come to visit
41. Being at a party where I hardly know anyone
42. Going to the movies with someone
43. Playing competitive team sports (softball, basketball, etc.)
44. Going to lectures or hearing speakers
45. Engaging in recreational sports with someone (tennis, bowling, skiing, etc.)
46. Attending a concert, play, opera, or ballet

TABLE 8–2

Social Activity Scores: Normal Range	
Comfort	150–198
Frequency	75–95

Overcoming Social-Participation Problems

We have already encouraged you to turn to Chapter 5 if you scored in the "anxious" range on your *comfort score*. This chapter assumes that your problems, like Janet's in the initial case illustration, are a result of faulty life planning, not anxiety.

There are two main planning problems that often interfere with social activity. We will refer to them as "inadequate stimulation" and "inadequate reward."

INADEQUATE STIMULATION

This label applies to situations where you fall into a routine that doesn't provide you with *easy opportunities* to do things with other people. This can happen in lots of ways; the following are just some of the possibilities:

- –You are tired from work in the evening and turn on the TV because it is the easiest thing to do.
- –You aren't being invited out by friends and don't get around to inviting them yourself.
- –You aren't working outside your home, or your job doesn't put you in contact with other people.
- –You work odd or irregular hours, so you can't easily plan activities with others.
- –Your work requires you to travel a lot, so you have trouble maintaining a group of friends in one place.
- –You have taken on a role, such as caring for a relative or chauffeuring for your children, that has occupied all of your spare time.
- –You don't pay attention to the entertainment section of your newspaper, so you never know what activities are happening in your area.
- –You got used to being close to one particular person, and now that person has moved away.

The list could go and on, but you probably have gotten the idea by now. What all of these possibilities have in common is that no active effort is being made to plan or create pleasant social interactions. In addition, for some of the items effort is being directed into activities that actually interfere with social interactions. It is difficult to plan ahead when you have other demands on your time or when you are not used to planning, but that effort may be just what you need to create a more active life and positive outlook.

The first thing you should do when you begin working on this problem is to go back to the items you filled out at the start of this chapter. Go through the items and find all the ones you marked as potentially enjoyable (that is, all the items to which you assigned 4 or 5 for comfort) but which you rarely do (that is, you gave the items a 1 or 2 for frequency). Write each of these activities down on the Social Activities to Increase form provided in Figure 8–1. Add to this sheet any activities that are not on the questionnaire and which you would like to do more often. Make the list as long as you want; you don't have to fill in all 20 spaces. You may want to copy the form and keep it in a conspicuous place (like your refrigerator door).* Doing the activities you have listed can *get you out of your rut*. You need to make some specific plans to start including more of these activities in your life. A sample form is filled out in Figure 8–2.

---

*So that you can make additional copies if you wish, the Social Activities to Increase form is included in the section titled *Extra Forms*, beginning on page 211.

FIGURE 8–1
Social Activities to Increase

Item	Date:								
1.									
2.									
3.									
4.									
5.									
6.									
7.									
8.									
9.									
10.									
11.									
12.									
13.									
14.									
15.									
16.									
17.									
18.									
19.									
20.									
Daily Totals:									

Month: _____

Goal for Increasing: _____ per _____ .

Average Increase Achieved: _____ per _____ .

FIGURE 8–2
Social Activities to Increase/Example

Item Date:	Month: January						
	9	10	11	12	13	14	15
1. Talking with a friend							
2. Going to an office party							
3. Accepting a social invitation							
4. Inviting a friend to join me for an activity							
5. Going to a service club meeting							
6. Talking with someone on the job							
7. Joining a friend for a social activity							
8. Giving a party							
9. Calling a friend on the telephone							
10. Having friends come to visit							
11. Going to the movies with someone							
12. Engaging in recreational sports with someone							
13. Attending a concert or ballet							
14. Introducing myself to neighbors							
15. Going on a picnic							
16.							
17.							
18.							
19.							
20.							
Daily Totals:							

Goal for Increasing: __4__ per __week__ .

Average Increase Achieved: _____ per _____ .

It might be helpful for you to make another list to show the bad habits you have developed that interfere with sharing interesting activities with other people. You will have to generate this list yourself, because we do not have a test that lists all the possibilities. To get started, think about how much time you spent watching TV, doing things for others that they could easily do for themselves (like picking up your children's toys), complaining, or sitting and feeling blue. On the next self-monitoring data sheet (Figure 8–3), list any of these things that apply to you, and then go on to think of more things that are especially time-consuming, unnecessary, and disrupting for you. You can list as many as you want; it isn't necessary to fill all 20 spaces.

These are the activities that could *keep you in your rut*. It is important for you to make some specific plans to start spending less of your time doing these things. Again, you may want to copy this form and post it by your list of activities that you want to do more often.* Figure 8–4 shows an example of this sheet filled out.

To help you turn these lists into practical plans, we urge you to follow this sequence:

1. Do all of the things already suggested in this chapter (fill out the Social Activity Questionnaire in Table 8–1 and use it to make a personalized list of social activities to increase, and create your own list of interfering activities).

2. You will now want to begin increasing your pleasant social activities. Each day, keep track of when each item occurs and mark it on your self-monitoring forms. On the Social Activities to Increase Form (Figure 8–1), put a check mark each day for each item that occurred and was at least slightly enjoyable. At the bottom of the sheet, add up and record your daily total. On the Interferences—Activities to Decrease Form (Figure 8–3), put a check mark each day for each item that occurred. At the bottom, add up and record your daily total. Your goal is to begin gradually increasing your enjoyable social interactions and decreasing your interfering activities. As you do this, notice your daily mood in relation to your daily activities. You can expect to see your mood getting better when your interferences go down and your social activities go up.

   The optimal level for each of these items varies a lot from person to person. You need to experiment and find the best mix for you. You probably don't want to spend all your time on pleasant socializing; many of those interfering activities may be important responsibilities you take seriously. Keep in mind that you are experimenting; you want to find a balance of pleasure and responsibility that works for you—that is, a level at which you feel happy instead of depressed.

---

*So that you can make additional copies if you wish, this form is included in the section titled *Extra Forms*, beginning on page 211.

FIGURE 8–3
Interferences: Activities to Decrease

Item	Date:							
1.								
2.								
3.								
4.								
5.								
6.								
7.								
8.								
9.								
10.								
11.								
12.								
13.								
14.								
15.								
16.								
17.								
18.								
19.								
20.								
Daily Totals:								

Month: _____

Goal for Decreasing: _____ per _____ .

Average Decrease Achieved: _____ per _____ .

FIGURE 8–4
**Interferences: Activities
to Decrease/Example**

Item	Date:	9	10	11	12	13	14	15
1. Ironing sheets								
2. Going to visit Aunt Jane at rest home								
3. Driving Susie places she could easily walk to								
4. Picking up Jimmy's room								
5. Waiting at home in case Susie needs a ride								
6. Complaining about Jimmy and Susie								
7. Watching daytime TV								
8. Reading movie magazines								
9. Baking cookies								
10. Afternoon "slump"								
11.								
12.								
13.								
14.								
15.								
16.								
17.								
18.								
19.								
20.								
Daily Totals:								

Month: ___January___

Goal for Decreasing: __1__ per __day__ .

Average Decrease Achieved: _____ per _____ .

To get started on your experiment, set a goal for increasing social activities; for example, you might try to increase your number of social activities by one per day or by three per week. Set your goal, and then *stick to it*. Write your goal at the bottom of the self-monitoring sheet (Figure 8–1).

Next, set a goal for decreasing interfering activities and write it at the bottom of Figure 8–3. Again, set your own goal, but try to stick to whatever you set up.

3. Learn how to gather information about social activities in your area. Many of the activities on your list may require knowledge about your community. For instance, "going on a recreational outing" may be easier if you know where to rent a canoe or what groups plan hikes together. Similarly, it will be easier to find an opportunity for "singing in a group" if you know about choirs, glee clubs, and musical comedy theater groups in your area. All of this information can be readily obtained by carefully reading your local newspaper. Most papers have one or two particular days when they provide a detailed list of all the group activities in the area, along with information on how to contact each group. If you don't know what day your paper features this column, call the office of the paper and ask. They will be glad to provide you with that information. Other suggestions for gathering information can be found at the end of Chapter 7.

4. In addition to following all the preceding steps, be sure to read the next section, *Inadequate Reward*. You may want to incorporate its suggestions in your plan.

INADEQUATE REWARD

Throughout this book we have emphasized the importance of rewarding yourself, especially when you are trying to change your behavior. The same message applies, just as powerfully, in the area of social participation. The joy of doing things with friends may eventually be all the reward you need, but as you begin trying to change, you will need some additional, more tangible rewards to help you maintain your resolve. The following list contains just some of the reasons why you should reward yourself:

–You may experience a few failures after you get started; people may turn down your invitations, or a party might be dull, or a restaurant you have chosen may be closed.

–It takes energy to get started; if you're used to doing things the easy way (for example, watching TV by yourself), you'll need a boost to help you get going.

–You may need to do some difficult things in order to arrange time for social activities (for example, telling your mother you won't be spending every afternoon with her anymore, or refusing to take on extra work on your job). You will need to reward yourself, or else the immediate difficulty of those steps may be more powerful than the long-range rewards you hope to gain.

These are just examples of reasons why self-reward is important; in your case, there may be a number of additional reasons. The important thing is to recognize that you are making an *effort* when you try to change, and efforts have to be rewarded if they are to be successful.

What if you have tried giving yourself rewards, and you have increased your social activities, but you find that social interaction is not turning out to be very rewarding? The things we have suggested in this chapter are based on the assumption that social activity will be pleasurable *in itself* once you get started. You may need external rewards to get going, but usually social interaction doesn't need extra rewards once you become more active.

However, for some people this is not the case. You may find that you feel it is unpleasant to be with others, or you may have recurring fears of rejection, or you may find that you are tense during and after a social interaction. This brings us full circle, back to the start of this chapter; you may need to reexamine your definition of the problem. If you feel anxious when you are among people, Chapter 5 can help you learn to relax. Chapter 7 can help if you are uncomfortable because you lack social skills. If you are comfortable with other people and your social behavior is pleasant and skillful, then you will find social interactions to be intrinsically rewarding. If social behavior does not provide adequate reward for you, back up and decide whether Chapter 5 or 7 might help. If you feel that those chapters will not be helpful but you really don't *enjoy* social interaction, you might want to discuss your problem with a counselor.

Monitoring Your Progress

It is important for you to keep track of your success as you work on this chapter. The easiest way to do that is to keep track *every day* of how many of the social activities on your personal list you are actually doing. Keep each day's records close at hand and compare them at the end of the week. If your plan is working, the number of activities should be gradually, but steadily, increasing according to the goal you have set. Of course, the number will fluctuate up and down a little, but on the whole you should look for slow, steady progress. If this is not happening, you need to reevaluate your plan and try again. If you find that you need to reevaluate your plan, the following checklist may help:

–Have you decreased the amount of time spent on interfering activities?

–Have you been rewarding yourself for small steps?

–Have you been gathering information about available social activities to help you carry out your plans?

–Have you set your goals in reasonable, small, steady steps?

–Have you given the plan enough time (at least three weeks)?

Use the information from the checklist to help you modify your plan to make it more effective.

A Sample Success Story

To give you an idea of how this plan can work, consider how Janet, the woman who was introduced at the beginning of this chapter, used this chapter to help overcome her depression:

Janet decided to do something about her rut. She worked out the following list of social activities:

SOCIAL ACTIVITIES TO INCREASE

1. Talking with a friend
2. Going on a recreational outing
3. Visiting friends
4. Dancing
5. Having lunch with friends
6. Going to a party
7. Giving a party or get-together
8. Having sexual relations with my husband
9. Going to the movies
10. Engaging in recreational sports with someone

She also worked out the following list of interfering activities:

INTERFERENCES: ACTIVITIES TO DECREASE

1. Doing the wash every day; twice a week would be plenty
2. Baking "goodies" too often—it takes time and we don't need the calories
3. Being "on call" constantly for the baby; he could stay at a day care center or with my mother three mornings a week so that I have time to do something special
4. Sitting around feeling sorry for myself! I wasted three evenings that way last week

Janet then set up a plan to help herself change. She wanted to increase her social activities by three each week. She found out about a hiking group in her area and joined it. She and her husband scheduled one night a week for activities outside the home, and decided to alternate between going to the movies, dancing, and going bowling. Janet made an effort to call friends and ask them over during the day, especially on the mornings when her son was at the day care center. Janet and her husband hosted a buffet dinner for a lot of friends with whom they had lost touch, and as a result more invitations were extended to them. As Janet became more active and happy, she and her husband became happier with each other. They had more to talk about, and their sex life improved, also.

Obviously, not all of these things happened right away. Janet kept track, and found that in the first two weeks she increased the activities on her list each week by only one or two. She kept at it, however, and by the end of four weeks she was keeping up with her weekly goal. After that, she felt much happier and more energetic and found that she was able to do more and more. By the end of two months, she had stabilized at doing fifteen of the activities on the list each week. That averages out to be about two activities per day (but actually, her pattern was to do about one activity per day during the weekdays, and the rest on weekends). Janet was also able to decrease her interfering activities. She arranged to have care for her baby, which immediately brought about a decrease of three interfering activities per week. In addition, she set a goal of decreasing the other interfering activities by one per week until they were down to a weekly total of four. She was able to accomplish that in a month.

Janet was very pleased with the pattern she had established after two months, and she no longer felt depressed. She stopped using her lists and plan at that point, but carefully put them away so that she could bring them out and use them again if she fell back into her old rut.

Janet is just one person, of course, but she illustrates what *you* can accomplish. If you try to use the chapter suggestions contained in this chapter, you may well create an actual success story much like Janet's. If you find that these suggestions don't work, however, remember that you should not despair. Not everyone improves at the same rate or using the same methods. Your depression will improve when you find the right approach for *you*.

SUMMARY

The chapter has set out a systematic approach for you to use to increase your social activities. It gives a step-by-step method to assess your difficulties, to set up a self-monitoring program, and to work on gradual increases in pleasant interactions with others. It also features some suggestions about how to use other sections of this book if you are anxious in social situations or if you need help gathering information while you work on increasing social activities.

REVIEW

☐ I have filled out the Social Activities Questionnaire (Table 8–1) and figured out my scores.

☐ I have decided whether I should work on this chapter, the relaxation chapter, or both.

☐ If I am working on this chapter, I have done the following things:

    ☐ I have made a list of social activities that I need to increase (Figure 8–2).

    ☐ I have made a list of interfering activities that I need to decrease (Figure 8–3).

    ☐ I am keeping track of the activities on both lists every day.

    ☐ I have set a goal for increasing social activities and a goal for decreasing interfering activities.

    ☐ I am systematically working toward reaching the goals I have set.

    ☐ I am using self-rewards to help motivate myself with the effort to change.

☐ I know what to do if I am not enjoying social activities. I shall do one of the following things:

    ☐ Use Chapter 5 to decrease my social anxiety.

    ☐ Use Chapter 7 to increase my social skill.

    ☐ See a counselor.

    ☐ Other:_____

☐ I have evaluated my progress at least once.

𝟡
Controlling Thoughts

Theresa, a 42-year-old woman, single-handedly reared her two children, David, now 16, and Lydia, 20 years old. The children's father left the family when they were very young, and Theresa had to struggle to provide for herself and the children. She managed to get a job as a secretary, despite the fact that she had not worked before, and now has her house almost paid for. For the past two years, she has had frequent crying spells, and her ability to attend to her job and her home has suffered somewhat. She feels overwhelmed by her duties.

According to Theresa, her activities at home and work have not changed much in the last few years. But since Lydia graduated from high school, Theresa has begun to think more and more that her life is nearly over. She repeatedly tells herself that the only thing she is good at is rearing children, cooking and cleaning for them, and providing them with a home. Once they leave, she will feel that her job has been done and she could die without being missed. At times she even questions her competence as a mother. She blames herself for her husband's dissatisfaction and wonders whether she should have remarried to provide the children with a father. She worries about her daughter's plans to marry her boyfriend. She thinks they won't be happy together and wonders whether Lydia just wants to leave home. David has become less communicative lately, and Theresa berates herself for not having been more available to him—maybe if she hadn't had to work, he would have learned to feel closer to her. She is continually wondering whether she'll be able to help David with college expenses or whether he, like Lydia, will choose not to continue his education.

Theresa's head is constantly filled with fears of tragedies, with self-blame about choices she made in the past, and with other negative thoughts. This kind of thinking is extremely destructive, energy-draining, and a source of much suffering. Yet she does not consider her thoughts as contributors to her depression. As far as she is concerned, they are merely a natural reflection of her difficult situation.

This chapter focuses on thoughts, their effect on depression, and ways in which you can learn to use thoughts to your advantage. The chapter will help you to do the following:

1. Become aware of specific thoughts, so that you can identify troublesome thoughts and beneficial thoughts.
2. Learn techniques to channel your thoughts into directions you decide are most appropriate at the moment.

Thoughts are especially good to work with for two reasons:

1. They are always with you. You can work with them anytime, anywhere.
2. They are pretty much under your control and no one else's. No one can directly change the way *you* think.

However, these characteristics of thoughts can also be disadvantageous for the following reasons:

1. *Because* they are always with you, you have learned to take thoughts for granted. It will be difficult for you to pay attention to them and take the need to change them seriously. Unless you seriously listen to your thoughts, you won't be able to change them.
2. *Because* your thoughts are only known to *you*, there is no way anyone else but you can directly observe whether they are changing. This means that you will have to be very conscientious about doing the exercises that are featured here in order to change the way you think. Only you will be able to tell whether or not you are applying what you have learned.

There is one thought you may need to consider before we get started. Many people who experience depression think of themselves as having an "illness" that must be "cured." This is one way of thinking about depression. An alternate way to think about it (and the way on which this book is based) is to see depression as an experience produced by the way you have *learned* to think, act, and feel. Therefore, in order to deal with depression, you need to think of yourself as actively learning new ways to think, act, and feel. As you learn new patterns of thought and behavior, you will begin to feel less depressed.

Self-Assessment of Thinking Patterns

In one of our studies we asked both depressed and nondepressed people to rate how often they had certain thoughts. We then picked the thoughts that were rated significantly differently by depressed and nondepressed people. They are presented here.

Indicate whether you have experienced each of the following thoughts in the past month by placing a check mark next to the appropriate thought.

SET A

- ☐ Life is interesting.
- ☐ I really feel great
- ☐ This is fun.
- ☐ I have great hopes for the future.
- ☐ I have good self-control.
- ☐ That's interesting.
- ☐ A nice, relaxing evening can sure be enjoyable.
- ☐ I have enough time to accomplish the things I most want to do.
- ☐ I like people.
- ☐ I'm pretty lucky.
- ☐ That's funny (humorous).
- ☐ I don't want to miss that event.
- ☐ *Total sum for Set A* (Highest possible score is 12)

SET B

- ☐ I'll always be sexually frustrated.
- ☐ I'm confused.
- ☐ There is no love in the world.
- ☐ I am wasting my life.
- ☐ I'm scared.
- ☐ Nobody loves me.
- ☐ I'll end up living all alone.
- ☐ People don't consider friendship important anymore.
- ☐ I don't have any patience.
- ☐ What's the use?
- ☐ That was a dumb thing for me to do.
- ☐ I'll probably have to be placed in a mental institution someday.
- ☐ Anybody who thinks I'm nice doesn't know the real me.
- ☐ Existence has no meaning, *or* life has no meaning.
- ☐ I am ugly.
- ☐ I can't express my feelings.
- ☐ I'll never find what I really want.
- ☐ I am not capable of loving.
- ☐ I am worthless.
- ☐ It's all my fault.
- ☐ Why do so many bad things happen to me?
- ☐ I can't think of anything that would be fun to do.
- ☐ I don't have what it takes.
- ☐ Bringing kids into the world is cruel because life isn't worth living.
- ☐ I'll never get over this depression.
- ☐ Things are so messed up that doing anything about them is futile.
- ☐ I don't have enough willpower.

☐ Why even bother getting up?
☐ I wish I were dead.
☐ I wonder if they are talking about me.
☐ Things are just going to get worse and worse.
☐ I have a bad temper.
☐ No matter how hard one tries, people aren't satisfied.
☐ Life is unfair.
☐ I'll never make good friends.
☐ I don't dare imagine what my life will be like in 10 years.
☐ There is something wrong with me.
☐ I am selfish.
☐ My memory is lousy.
☐ I am not as good as so-and-so.
☐ My feelings are hurt easily.
☐ *Total sum for Set B* (Highest possible score is 41)

Now summarize your results as follows:

Positive thoughts (Set A Total): _____
Negative thoughts (Set B Total): _____
Ratio of positive to negative thoughts (Set A Total ÷ Set B Total): _____

If your ratio is less than 2, you can profit from putting into practice the techniques explained in this chapter.

Mr. Jackson checked 2 thoughts from Set A and 16 from Set B. His ratio was 2 ÷ 16 = 0.125. He therefore decided to read and put into practice the exercises outlined in this chapter.

Mr. Hall checked 10 thoughts from Set A and 3 from Set B. His ratio was 10 ÷ 3 = 3.33. He decided to work on another chapter but read this chapter out of curiosity.

Identifying Thoughts

When you begin to work with thoughts, you need to learn to identify them. A fairly easy way to do this is to begin to keep track of "positive" and "negative" thoughts. Positive thoughts are those thoughts that have a positive effect on your mood and reflect the good points of whatever they refer to. For example, they may reflect your good characteristics ("I am intelligent," "I am dependable," "I know how to enjoy myself"). Or they may reflect the good parts of your life ("My family is great," "My work is satisfying," "Our health is good"). Negative thoughts are those thoughts that have a negative effect on your mood, usually because they focus on bad points ("I am worthless," "I can't do anything right," "My wife is a nag," "My husband is lazy").

DIRECTIONS

1. Using a 3″ by 5″ card, label one side of the card with a plus sign ("+" for positive thoughts) and the other side with a minus sign ("−" for negative thoughts). Use one card per day and date it.
2. Jot down positive and negative thoughts on the appropriate side of the card as soon after you think them as possible. (If you have trouble remembering to do this, make it a habit to take a few minutes before breakfast, lunch, dinner, and bedtime to jot down the important positive and negative thoughts of the last few hours.)

Below are examples of these cards.

+   Date _____

I really feel great
That's interesting
I have great hopes for the future
I like people
A nice, relaxing evening can sure be enjoyable

−   Date _____

I am worthless
Can't think of anything that could be fun
I am not capable of loving
I'll never get over this depression
Nobody loves me
There is something wrong with me

You won't be able to write down *every* thought you have, of course. If you can write down 10 positive thoughts and 10 negative thoughts each day, you'll be doing well. By the end of a week, you will have a good sample of positive and negative thoughts. You may find that some thoughts occur to you repeatedly, that some are more disturbing than others, and, in general, that some thoughts seem to be particularly powerful in influencing your mood.

Make a personalized list of the most important thoughts you have found during your week's self-observation (see Figure 9–2). Place a star next to those thoughts that are particularly helpful to you in regard to your mood. If you remember important thoughts you had that were not included on the list, add them later on. You may want to refer to the lists in Set A and Set B that were covered earlier in this chapter.

FIGURE 9–2
Inventory of Thoughts

Negative	Positive

Counting Thoughts

Now that you have identified the kinds of thoughts that are most likely to occur to you, it will be easier to count them.

For one week, tally each positive thought and each negative thought as it occurs during the day. Again label your 3″ by 5″ card with a " + " on one side and a " − " on the other. Total your tally marks at the end of each day and record your totals on the form provided in Figure 9–3.

FIGURE 9–3

	Number of Negative Thoughts	Number of Positive Thoughts
Day 1	_____	_____
Day 2	_____	_____
Day 3	_____	_____
Day 4	_____	_____
Day 5	_____	_____
Day 6	_____	_____
Day 7	_____	_____
Total for the week	_____	_____
Average for the week	_____	_____

These are your "Base-line" averages.

If your average number of negative thoughts is greater than your average number of positive thoughts, continue to read this chapter. If your average number of positive thoughts is greater than your average number of negative thoughts, you may already be changing your thinking patterns. In this case, you may want to skip this chapter. Before you do, however, it's a good idea to skim through it and read the summary at the end of the chapter.

Managing Thoughts:
Decreasing Negative Thinking

When you are depressed, you tend to have a higher number of negative thoughts than when you are not depressed. These thoughts, which may have been originally caused by feelings of depression, in turn produce more depressed feelings, thus starting a destructive downward spiral. By breaking up this process, you can reduce feelings of depression and get yourself back into a more pleasant state of mind.

The following three techniques have been found to be helpful in controlling negative thoughts. Choose one of the techniques and try it for one week, keeping a tally of the number of negative thoughts you have each day. If at the end of the week your average is less than your baseline average, the technique is working. If it is not, you should switch to another technique and test *it* for one week. Do not give up on a technique without giving it reasonable time to work for you.

THOUGHT INTERRUPTION

As soon as you notice that you are producing a negative thought, interrupt the thought and return to whatever non-negative thoughts you were having. In order to interrupt a negative thought, instruct yourself as follows: "I am going to stop thinking about that now." Then, without getting upset, let your attention flow back into non-negative ideas. This is probably the easiest interruption method, and the one we recommend most highly. There are two other methods that have been found to be useful by some people and which bear mentioning.

One method involves a stronger interruption. You should begin practicing this method someplace where you are not likely to be heard (for example, when you are home alone or when you are driving by yourself). When you are ready to begin, start thinking a negative thought and, as soon as you are certain that the thought is clearly in your mind, yell the word "STOP!" as loudly as you can. You'll notice that the negative thought will be pushed aside for a few seconds by the very force of the act of yelling. At this point, direct your attention toward thinking non-negative thoughts. Repeat the actual yelling technique for about three days; then begin reducing the volume of the yell, while at the same time maintaining the force behind it. Continue this process until you can "yell" the word "STOP!" mentally, feeling the full force of the yell without making a sound. Now you are ready to use the technique in public.

The third technique originates from the notion that an act that is punished consistently will occur less and less frequently. In this case, the act is the negative thought. The punishment is a "slap on the wrist" with a rubber band. Specifically, you begin by wearing a heavy-gauge rubber band around your wrist. As soon as you notice a negative thought, you snap the band against your wrist. If you do this consistently, you will soon begin to catch negative thoughts almost as soon as they begin, and the frequency of such thoughts will drop.

For all three of these techniques, remember to record your positive and negative thoughts and inspect the record regularly to ascertain whether the negative thoughts are diminishing. Choose one of the three interruption methods now, and practice it for the next week. Remember to record your positive and negative thoughts.

WORRYING TIME

One of the many sources of depression is an inability to keep certain negative thoughts away. These thoughts may be particularly bothersome ideas that intrude into your train of thought again and again, draining your energy and distracting you from the task at hand. This is sometimes called "obsessive thinking." If you feel that you need to spend some time mulling these thoughts over, the technique outlined here is exactly what you need. Decide how long you think you should spend on these intrusive but necessary thoughts and then schedule them into you day. Do not allow these thoughts to interfere with your mood or your work or play at any other time. If you feel that it is difficult for you to set aside a thought completely when it occurs for fear that you may not remember to think about it during your "worrying time," then keep a pen or pencil and paper handy to jot down a word or two that will remind you of particularly important thoughts.

The point of this technique is not to avoid thinking about unpleasant subjects completely. Rather, it is to let you decide *when* the best time is to turn your attention to what you consider necessary thinking, and to free you from having to constantly carry your mental burdens with you. One half hour of worrying time a day usually proves sufficient for most people. The technique works best if you refrain from doing anything else except thinking during your "worrying time." For example, select one particular chair in which to sit and think—without talking, eating, drinking, working, or playing. Just knowing that you have set aside a daily "worrying time" may make it easier to forego ruminating over worries at other times.

Fill in: My worrying time will start at _____ o'clock and last _____ minutes.

Note: If you use this technique, tally only negative thoughts that occur *outside* of your "worrying time" in your daily total.

THE BLOW-UP TECHNIQUE

This is a technique designed to reduce the impact of a disturbing negative thought by exaggerating it beyond all proportion, thus making it so ridiculous that it ceases to be fearful.

> Marsha had been worried about having to tell her supervisor that she had made a major error on an order she had taken care of at the shipping department of a major store. But, in order to correct her error, she *had* to tell her. She fretted about it for a few days, lost some sleep over it, and became so quiet at work that one of her co-workers became concerned that something was wrong.

Marsha realized then that she couldn't put off speaking to her supervisor any longer, and began to ask herself why she was so fearful about discussing her mistake with her supervisor. She decided that she was afraid of having the supervisor think that she was incompetent, and would perhaps tell her co-workers, who would then also consider Marsha stupid or careless.

The way Marsha used the blow-up technique was to imagine that her supervisor became terribly upset at her error—she began screaming at the top of her lungs, throwing objects at Marsha, and stomping up and down on the resulting wreckage. Marsha's co-workers heard the commotion and joined in on the ruckus. They finally placed a big sign on Marsha's chest which read "STUPID" and outfitted her with a "dunce" cap. The store's loudspeaker blared out Marsha's error throughout the day, and as Marsha rode on the bus (with her cap and sign still on) she could see headlines proclaiming her error on the newspapers being read by the bus riders. The people in the streets booed her, and little children stuck out their tongues at her.

Marsha found the process of letting her imagination run wild somewhat funny. The ridiculous flavor of her exaggerated images blended with her earlier fear of telling her supervisor, giving the situation a less threatening tone.

She went ahead and talked with her supervisor . . . and survived!

Managing Thoughts: Increasing Positive Thinking

Reducing the number of negative thoughts you have will not automatically increase the number of positive thoughts. You need to learn techniques designed to accomplish each of these objectives.

In order to increase the number of positive thoughts you generate, choose one of the following techniques and keep a daily count of positive thoughts you have for one week. If your average for that week is greater than your base-line average, you will know that the technique is working. If the average is less, choose another technique and test its effectiveness for a week.

PRIMING

Priming is a technique designed to increase positive thoughts. Its name comes from the phrase "priming the pump" (which originally meant placing water in the barrel of a dry pump to begin the pumping action that would start the desired flow of water). In our case, the word refers to systematically placing positive thoughts in your mind so that you can break the pattern of thinking negative thoughts and can thus start the flow of positive thoughts.

First, you need to put together a list of positive thoughts. Use the list in Set A, which appears earlier in this chapter. Add any thoughts you came up with to your index cards. Push yourself to add still more. Think especially about thoughts that refer to *yourself*. If necessary, ask people you trust to tell you what they consider your good points.

Second, write down these thoughts on 3″ by 5″ cards, one thought per card. You will then have a deck of positive thoughts.

Third, begin to prime your "positive thought pump" by carrying the deck of cards with you; pull a card out at different times throughout the day and read it, paying serious attention to it.

Add new positive thoughts about yourself to the deck as the thoughts occur to you. Also, begin placing "wild cards" in the deck. When you get to a card labeled "wild card," you must generate a positive thought about yourself on the spot. This will help you to begin to formulate positive thoughts on your own.

USING CUES

Use frequent behaviors to remind yourself to have a positive thought. Because positive thoughts don't occur very frequently in your present daily routine, you can increase their frequency by pairing them to things you do often.

For example, remind yourself to think a positive thought each time you eat, brush your teeth, talk on the phone, read something, get in your car or on the bus, and so on.

NOTICING WHAT YOU ACCOMPLISH

Many depressed people don't give themselves credit for what they do. Instead, they belittle themselves when something doesn't work out right.

To see if this is true in your case, begin to keep track of all the things you accomplish during the day—even things you may consider to be trivial. Carry a few 3″ by 5″ cards with you and jot down every task you complete throughout the day. A typical list may look like this:

Got up on time.
Cooked and ate a nutritious breakfast.
Dressed neatly.
Got to work on time.
Conducted myself properly at a meeting with my boss.
Finished a project.
Planned an effective schedule for the day
Selected a nice place for lunch.
Had a good conversation with a co-worker.
Accomplished three out of the five things I wanted to finish today.
Drove home skillfully—didn't let traffic get me angry.
Cooked a good dinner.
Saw a TV program I really wanted to see.

The object of this technique is to observe what you do during your day. Many people feel that they don't do anything when, in fact, their days are full of activities for which they don't give themselves credit.

POSITIVE SELF-REWARDING THOUGHTS

It usually makes us feel good to hear someone tell us they appreciate what we have done. We feel good when our contribution is noticed, our efforts are considered worthwhile, and our value is acknowledged. These three elements can also be present within our own thoughts.

The result of being praised or encouraged is usually an increase in the desire to continue to do well. You too can produce a similar effect by praising or encouraging yourself.

If you were to tell other people that they are lazy or incompetent, or that their work is unimportant or lousy, they would probably be less likely to feel good about themselves or their efforts. They might give up and stop trying. The same result can take place if you tell yourself those things.

Because one of the problems depressed persons have is that they don't do much, it makes sense to notice if you are encouraging this inactivity by punishing yourself with negative thoughts before, during, or after you do something. For example, when you *consider* getting together with friends, do you think to yourself, "It will be boring" or "I really don't feel like it"? *During* an outing or a visit, do you say to yourself, "I don't fit in here" or "Everyone is looking at me"? *After* you have done something you were looking forward to doing, do you come down hard on yourself and focus on all the disappointing parts of the experience instead of enjoying the fact that you finally did it? Do you think, for example, "I really could have done a lot better," "I looked like a fool," or "No one really enjoyed it?"

By increasing your level of positive self-reward, you can increase your level of activities and your level of positive thoughts. The trick is to reward yourself silently after you do or think something positive by "patting yourself on the back." For example, let's say you are considering getting together with friends, and you could think to yourself: "That's a constructive idea. Having this type of idea means I am making progress. I am headed in the right direction." Or during an outing you might think: "I haven't done this for so long. It took guts to try it. I am proud of myself." And, afterward: "I did it! I really did it! Not bad!"

We have found that many people are reluctant to praise themselves because they see that as being too proud, or egotistical, or self-centered. The fact is that *all of us need encouragement.* If it is good to compliment other people for good work, then it certainly makes sense to do the same for oneself.

TIME PROJECTION

One of the most frightening things about depression is that while you are thinking, feeling, and acting depressed, you believe that the state you are in is never going to end. The time projection technique breaks through this tendency by having you mentally travel forward in time far enough so that, in your estimation, the stressful period has ended.

The stessful period may be as short as a visit to the dentist or as long as a period of mourning. In the first case, for example, the idea is to acknowledge the anxiety and discomfort you are experiencing in the dentist's chair; and then "jump forward" in time a couple of hours to when the only discomfort will possibly be a residual numbness from the anesthetic; and then again a week or so later, when you won't even be thinking about the fact that you were at the dentist's today.

In the case of mourning or separation, you would acknowledge the memories, the loss, and the pain you now feel, and then think about the fact that the pain—which may be almost unbearable at times now—*must* decrease as time goes on, and that in a few months the memories of your loved one will be less burdened by the deep hurt or emptiness that you feel now.

Time projection can be used to help you survive a crisis, to produce hope of having your suffering alleviated, and to remind yourself that psychological pain is *not* fatal.

At the same time, we would like to underscore a basic concept often overlooked by many depressed people. Feelings of sadness, pain, depression are natural parts of life. They are experienced at all levels, from very minor to most intense. *It is OK to feel depressed.* Human beings can bear very intense levels of depressed feelings. It is only when you become demoralized, lose hope, and forget that you can endure the pain and go on living that the trouble starts. Time projection acknowledges the pain and helps you see a more satisfying future.

Evaluating Your Efforts

The goal of this chapter is to help you identify thoughts that make you depressed, learn to count them, and know how to control them.

To do this we have focused on negative thoughts—those thoughts that have a negative influence on your mood; and positive thoughts—those thoughts that have a positive influence on your mood. Your baseline averages can serve as a guide for your self-change project. Your goal is to increase the number of positive thoughts you have and decrease the number of negative thoughts you have until you have as many or more positive thoughts as negative thoughts each day. Recall the social learning concepts we mentioned in Chapter 2:

1. *Antecedents:* Note when and where you are most likely to have negative thoughts. Do you experience them when you are in certain places or with certain people, or at certain times of the day? If so, devise alternative plans for yourself so you can avoid or deal differently with these situations.
2. *Consequences:* Do you reward yourself for thinking negative thoughts? For example, do you let depressive thinking serve as an excuse for postponing an unpleasant chore?
3. *Mental factors:* Do you punish yourself mentally when you have positive thoughts? For example, do you label yourself conceited for thinking you do something well? Or do you belittle what you did and tell yourself you didn't really do it well enough?

Use the following self-change elements, also:

1. *Self-reward.* Reward yourself for putting these techniques into practice.
2. *Step-by-step change.* Notice small changes in your thinking. If you reduce your average negative thoughts by even one thought per week, you are being successful in your self-change program. Don't expect to experience no negative thoughts. That's not a realistic goal.
3. *Modeling.* Imagine how some nondepressed person you admire might think. Ask yourself how this person would deal with a negative thought. What kind of positive thoughts would this person come up with if he or she were in your shoes?
4. *Self-observation.* By keeping records, you make it easier to pay attention to your self-change project. This also helps you with self-reinforcement, because it gives you a clear picture of how much you are changing.

Thinking and Depression

The ways you have learned to think, act, and feel affect how likely you are likely to feel depressed. In order to control your feelings of depression, you need to *relearn* how to think, act, and feel.

Thinking affects feelings and actions. You can learn to think in constructive ways. In order to accomplish this, you need to learn to identify thoughts, count them, and modify them. In general, you want to stop distorting reality in a negative direction by beginning to focus on positive perspectives.

SUMMARY

This chapter explains how thoughts affect depression and how a person can learn to manage his or her own thoughts to deal effectively with depression. It includes an exercise for self-assessment of thinking patterns, techniques for identifying, counting, and managing thoughts, and a procedure for evaluating thoughts.

After reading this chapter, you should know how thoughts affect mood, how to decrease the frequency of negative thoughts, and how to increase the frequency of positive thoughts.

REVIEW

☐ I understand how a person's thoughts affect his/her mood.

☐ I have completed the *Self-Assessment of Thinking Patterns section.* My score was _____. This means the following:
    ☐ I needed to change my thinking.
    ☐ My ratio of positive to negative thoughts is OK as is.

☐ I used 3″ by 5″ cards to identify my positive and negative thoughts.

☐ I filled out the *Inventory of Thoughts* form (Figure 9–2).

☐ I counted my negative and positive thoughts daily for a week.

☐ I tried (for at least a week) the techniques called:
    ☐ Thought Interruption
    ☐ Worrying Time
    ☐ The Blow-Up Technique
    ☐ Priming
    ☐ Using Cues
    ☐ Noticing What I Accomplish
    ☐ Positive Self-Rewarding Thoughts
    ☐ Time Projection

10

Constructive Thinking

In the last chapter we discussed how thoughts are very closely connected with both feelings and actions. For some people, changing their thoughts or attitudes about problems and difficulties can be a helpful way to begin feeling less depressed. In this chapter we focus on ways to change the way you think about problems and difficulties so you will be less upset by them, and, therefore, can approach and deal with them more constructively.

In order to help you evaluate whether this chapter will be useful for you, we will begin with a test. For each of the 13 statements listed below, rate how much you agree or disagree using the following scale:

1 = I disagree completely
2 = I disagree slightly
3 = I am neutral about this statement
4 = I agree slightly
5 = I agree completely

There are no right or wrong answers. It is important that you rate each item according to what you really believe.

☐ Considering the blatant and widespread sexism in our society, it is unlikely that any concerned woman can be truly happy.

☐ Some people could not be happy living in a small town or a large city because some of the things they need are not available there.

☐ There are some people in this world who truly can be described as rotten.

☐ If things are not the way one would like them to be, it is a catastrophe.

☐ Given the kind of home life some people have had, it is almost impossible for them ever to be happy.

☐ What others think of you is most important.

☐ Persons living in slum conditions are almost certain to feel depressed or miserable.

☐ Love and success are two basic human needs.

☐ Avoiding life's difficulties and one's responsibilities is easier than facing them.

☐ The main goal and purpose of life is achievement and success.

☐ Failure at something one really wants to do is terrible.

☐ People really can't help it when they feel angry, depressed, or guilty.

☐ One should blame oneself severely for all mistakes and wrongdoing.

To score the test, add up all of your ratings. If you find that your score is higher than 39, then you are likely to find this chapter helpful. A high score indicates that you, like many people, may tend to overreact to problems and difficulties that occur in your day-to-day life. If your score was within or lower than the 27 to 39 range (the average range) but you feel you do have a tendency to overreact to problems, you might still find this chapter useful. You may however, choose to skip this chapter and go on to a different chapter.

Overreacting to Problems and Difficulties

What do we mean when we say you may overreact to problems and difficulties? Perhaps the following examples will illustrate what we have in mind:

Jack started taking night classes at the community college in his city. It had been quite some time since he finished high school, so learning to study and take notes in class was not very easy for him. He worked hard all semester, partly because his courses would help him get the certification he needs for a job promotion, but mostly because it has always been important to Jack to do well at whatever he does. His toughest class has been algebra, and he has been spending a lot of time preparing for the final exam. With the help of a tutor, he now feels quite confident that he can get an *A* on the exam. After taking the exam, he was sure he did well and told his tutor, his closest friend, and his boss that he thought he'd get an *A* in algebra. When he got the exam back, Jack was shocked to see that his grade was not an *A* or even a *B*, but a *C*. Jack was very upset and, at first, was sure there had to be a mistake, but he soon found out that the grade was indeed correct. He felt like a total failure, very discouraged and down. He figured he might as well give up on the idea of trying to earn more college credits because it seemed so obvious to him that he was too "dumb" to do the work.

Melanie came home late one afternoon. She had just returned from the beauty parlor, where she had had her hair cut in a new, different style.

Melanie thought she looked pretty good, but was anxious to see what Jim, her husband, thought. When Jim arrived home, he mixed himself his usual before-dinner drink and sat down with the newspaper. Melanie was disappointed that he didn't notice her hair but decided not to say anything. After a little while, Jim started talking to Melanie about his day at work. Melanie pretended to be listening but was becoming more and more upset that he hadn't said anything about her new haircut. Finally, she burst into tears and ran into the bedroom, slamming the door behind her. She was both very angry and very hurt. When Jim came to find out what was wrong, she yelled, "Go away!" and continued to sob.

Jan had just been out on her first date with Allan, a very handsome man who recently took a job at the office where she works. Jan had had a good time on their date and thought he had too. She hoped that Allan would ask her out again soon. The next day at work, she was chatting with John, a good friend of hers. Knowing that John and Allan talk with one another quite a bit, she asked John if Allan had said anything about her or their date. John hesitated and then said, "Well, I don't really know—I guess I don't think you ought to count on going out with him again." When Jan pressed him for more information, he said that the only thing Allan had said about their date was, "Jan's a nice person, but she's just not my type." Jan was upset to hear this, and the more she thought about it, the worse she felt. She now thinks of herself as an unattractive woman and feels unloved and unlovable. She decided that if she goes out at all in the future, it will have to be with men she doesn't really like very much. For the next several days, Jan felt very discouraged, lonely, and down.

All three of these people had unpleasant things happen to them. It is quite natural to feel disappointed in such circumstances. Certainly it would be unrealistic to expect Jack to not feel disappointed when he got a *C* instead of an *A* on his exam. Similarly, we wouldn't expect Melanie not to be annoyed about her husband's failure to comment on her haircut or Jan not to feel a little hurt when she learned that Allan wasn't as attracted to her as she had hoped. But their reactions went far beyond being disappointed or annoyed or "a little" hurt. Jack concluded that he was dumb and felt like a total failure. Melanie felt very angry and hurt and couldn't help her husband understand what was wrong. Jan decided she was an unattractive, unlovable woman and felt very down for several days. Each of these people overreacted, making it more difficult to constructively approach the problem situation.

Listed below are some of the kinds of situations that lead many people to overreact and become quite upset:

1. Being rejected by someone or realizing that someone doesn't care about you to the same degree that you care about him or her.
2. Being disapproved of or criticized by someone.

3. Feeling unappreciated by someone who has received quite a bit of your attention, caring, or effort.
4. Doing more than your share of work and not getting credit for it.
5. Failing at something, making a mistake, or doing something less skillfully than you think you should have.
6. Having someone *not* do or say something you think he/she should have done or said *or* having someone do or say something you think he/she should *not* have done or said.
7. Having things turn out differently from how you had expected or hoped.
8. Being unfairly accused of something you did not do.

Can you think of times when you have experienced one or more of these unpleasant events? On some of those occasions, did you overreact (that is, become excessively upset)?

The A-B-C Method

A well-known psychologist, Dr. Albert Ellis, has developed an approach for helping people learn to think more constructively about these kinds of difficulties.* He calls his approach "Rational-Emotive Therapy." It is a way of stressing the connection between what you think and how you feel. As part of this therapy, Dr. Ellis presents a fairly simple method to help people learn to identify the kinds of beliefs or attitudes they hold that may lead them to overreact to problems or difficulties.

Our suggested plan is based on Dr. Ellis' techniques and on the self-help method developed by Dr. Gerald Kranzler. The technique is called the A-B-C method. *A* stands for *Activating Event*, the event you feel upset about. For Jack, *A* = receiving a low grade on his exam. For Melanie, *A* = her husband's not commenting on her new haircut. For Jan, *A* = learning that Allan doesn't consider her "his type." For the moment, we will skip *B* and discuss *C*, which stands for *Emotional Consequences*. For Jack, *C* = feeling very upset and discouraged. For Melanie, C = feeling very angry and hurt. For Jan, C = feeling very hurt and down.

Most people assume that *A* causes *C*. If we asked Jack why he was so upset, he would probably say, "Because I got a low grade on my exam." Assuming that *A* causes *C* is often accurate if you are talking about physical pain. For example, if you stub your toe *(A)* and feel pain *(C)*, it is accurate to say that *A* caused *C*. But it is *not* accurate to say that *A* causes *C* when we talk about psychological pain. When you feel angry or

*Ellis, A., and Harper, R. A. *A Guide to Rational Living* (No. Hollywood, Calif.: Wilshire Book Co., 1973).

hurt or very down *(C)*, it is not *A* (the Activating Event) that causes your emotional reaction; rather, it is *B*, what you believe or say to yourself about *A*, that results in your emotional reaction *(C)*. It's your *interpretation (B)* of events *(A)* that leads to emotional upset *(C)*.

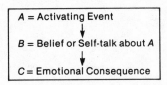

For Jack, *B* = his belief that he *should* have gotten a higher grade on his exam and that, since he didn't, he was a *total* failure and very dumb. For Melanie, *B* = telling herself that it was *awful* that her husband didn't notice and comment on her new haircut. For Jan, *B* = telling herself that it was terrible that Allan didn't think she was "his type" and that, since *he* didn't find her attractive, she *must be* very unattractive and unlovable.

In order to change the state of *C*, your emotional overreaction, you need to learn how to change *B*, the kinds of beliefs you hold or what you tell yourself about problems and difficulties that are bound to occur in everybody's life. The procedure we describe here is based upon the method described by Dr. Kranzler's booklet, *You Can Change How You Feel.**

Step 1 Turn to Section *C* on the form shown in 10–1 and briefly describe an unpleasant emotion you have experienced today. (It may be helpful to say to yourself, "I felt _____," and use a word such as "angry," "depressed," "guilty," "sad," "hurt," "used," "disgusted," "anxious," or "down" to complete the sentence.) Also, rate how upset you were, using a scale from 0 (only mildly upset) to 5 (extremely upset).

Step 2 In Section *A*, on the form, briefly describe the activating event, the situation or event that seemed to lead to your emotional reaction.

Step 3 As accurately as possible, list the kinds of things you are saying to yourself at point *B*. Place a check mark beside those statements that are *not* constructive or reasonable.

Step 3 may be difficult to do at first because the emotional consequences (*C*) generally follow the activating event (*A*) so automatically. Even though it is difficult at first, most people can learn to become aware of their self-talk at point *B*. Some of this self-talk is not constructive

---

*Kranzler, G. *You Can Change How You Feel* (Eugene, Ore.: University of Oregon Press, 1974).

FIGURE 10–1
Daily Monitoring Form

Daily Monitoring Form*

Date_____

A. Activating Event

(Briefly describe the situation or event that seemed to lead to your emotional upset at C.)

B. Beliefs or Self-Talk

(List each of the things you said to yourself about A.)

1.

2.

3.

4.

5.

(Now go back and place a check mark beside each statement that is nonconstructive or "irrational.")

C. Emotional Consequences

(Describe and rate how you felt when A happened.)

I felt:_____

_____

Rating (0 = mildly upset; 5 = extremely upset):_____

D. Dispute of Self-Talk

(For each checked statement in Section B, describe what you would ask or say to dispute your non-constructive self-talk.)

Note: You should first complete Section C. Then go back and complete Section A and Section B. After the first week of self-monitoring, also complete Section D.

because it almost guarantees that you are going to feel quite upset or bad. Dr. Kranzler lists three good indicators of nonconstructive self-talk:

1. *Highly evaluative words* like "should," "ought," or "must" (for example, he *ought* to say what I'd like him to say, or I *should* be able to do this well).
2. *Catastrophizing* words like "It's awful" or "It's terrible" or "I just can't stand it."
3. *Overgeneralizations*, such as "I'll never be able to do this" or "Nobody will ever like me" or "I'm really a bad or rotten person."

Of course, some of your self-talk at point *B* may be quite reasonable. Examples of reasonable self-talk are statements that begin with: "I wish . . ." or "I would have preferred . . ." or statements like "I am disappointed that . . ." or "I don't like . . ." Statements about your wishes, preferences, likes, and dislikes are perfectly reasonable. If that's *all* you are saying to yourself when an unpleasant situation occurs, you may feel annoyed or disappointed but you *won't* feel prolonged or intense hurt, sadness, anger, and so on.

For the next week, use the Daily Monitoring Form to keep track of your reactions and self-talk about *one* unpleasant event each day. At the end of each day, first complete Section *C*, then Section *A*, and then Section *B* on the form. For the time being, ignore Section *D*.*

Figures 10–2(a), (b), and (c) show the forms Jack, Melanie, and Jan filled out for the days on which the events we've described occurred.

After one week of self-monitoring, you should go on to Step 4, which follows. We suggest that you complete Sections *A*, *B*, and *C* for one situation per day for one week *before* continuing with the rest of this chapter.

FIGURE 10–2(a)
Jack's Daily Monitoring Form

A. Activating Event

Getting a C on my exam.

B. Beliefs or Self-Talk

✓1. *It's terrible that I didn't get an A.*
✓2. *I'm a total failure.*
✓3. *This shows how dumb I am.*
4.
5.

C. Emotional Consequences

I felt: *very upset*

Rating: *5*

---

*So that you can make additional copies for your daily monitoring, this form is included in the section titled *Extra Forms*, beginning on page 211.

FIGURE 10–2(b)
Melanie's Daily Monitoring Form

A. Activating Event
    Jim didn't say anything about my hair.

B. Beliefs or Self-Talk
    1. *I wish Jim had said something about my hair*
    ✓2. *Jim should have said something*
    ✓3. *It's terrible that he didn't*
    4.
    5.

C. Emotional Consequences
    I felt: _____ *very angry; hurt*

    Rating: __4__

FIGURE 10–2(c)
Jan's Daily Monitoring Form

A. Activating Event
    Allan said I wasn't his type.

B. Beliefs or Self-Talk
    ✓1. *It's awful that Allan doesn't like me.*
    ✓2. *I must be very unattractive.*
    ✓3. *Nobody will ever like me.*
    4. *I wish Allan would have liked me.*
    5.

C. Emotional Consequences
    I felt: _____ *upset & down; hurt*

    Rating: __5__

Disputing Your Nonconstructive Self-Talk

After one week of self-monitoring, you'll probably become more aware of the kinds of things you say to yourself at point *B* that lead to the emotional overreaction you experience at point *C*. Perhaps just becoming aware of some of your self-talk has helped you react more calmly to unpleasant situations or events in your day-to-day life. An additional helpful step is to dispute actively the things you say to yourself at point *B*. By disputing self-talk, we mean coming up with arguments to use against your "should" and "ought" statements, against your beliefs that certain things are "awful" or "terrible," and against your overgeneralizations—the "always" and "never" statements. Some examples of disputing follow:

For "shoulds" and "oughts":	*"Why* should I or the other person behave in this particular way?"
	"Why must an event occur just the way I wanted it
For "terribles" and "awfuls":	"I would have liked this person to do or say this, but is there any good reason why he (or she) must do or say what I'd like?"
	"I would have liked for this to have happened in a different way, but is it really *awful* (or *horrible* or *terrible*) that it didn't?
	"It would have been nice if that person had done or said this, but is it really *terrible* that he (or she) didn't?
For overgeneralizations:	"Just because this didn't work out the way I wanted, is there any good evidence that it can't work out better another time?"
	"Just because that person said something about me that I didn't like, does that really mean that everyone is going to feel that way?"

From now on, when you complete the daily monitoring form, be sure to complete Section *D*. For each of the nonconstructive things you said to yourself in Section *B* (the checked statements), write in Section *D* how you would dispute or argue against them. Examples for Jack, Melanie, and Jan are shown in Figures 10-3(a), (b), and (c).

As you complete Section *D*, follow our general guidelines but use your own words in disputing your self-talk. For practice, go back over your daily monitoring forms for the past week and complete Section *D*. From now on, complete all four sections for one situation each day: first, Section *C*, then *A*, then *B*, and finally, *D*.

You may soon notice that you are substituting constructive self-talk at point *B* and that your emotional consequences are less upsetting and/or take up less time. This, of course, is the goal for people using this approach. But don't worry if your progress seems slow at first. The self-talk most of us engage in at point *B* has developed over a number of years and operates much like an automatic habit. Like other habits that have had bad consequences (for example, smoking), such habits are not easy to change, and changing them requires much effort and patience. Even if

FIGURE 10–3(a)
Jack

> *D.* Dispute of Self-Talk
>
> 1. Sure I'm disappointed but is it really _terrible_ that I didn't get an A grade?
>
> 2. Does getting a C grade really mean I'm a _total_ failure?
>
> 3. Just because I'm not a real whiz at algebra, does that mean I'm _dumb_?

FIGURE 10–3(b)
Melanie

> *D.* Dispute of Self-Talk
>
> 1. OK (reasonable)
>
> 2. Yes, it would be nice if Jim had said something, I would have liked that. But is there any good reason why he _must_?
>
> 3. I was disappointed but is it really _terrible_ that he said nothing?

FIGURE 10–3(c)
Jan

> *D.* Dispute of Self-Talk
>
> 1. I would have liked it if Allan had liked me better but is it really _awful_ that he didn't?
>
> 2. Just because Allan didn't find me attractive, is that good evidence that I'm _unattractive_?
>
> 3. Just because Allan didn't like me does that really mean _nobody ever_ will?
>
> 4. OK (reasonable)

you realize afterward that you have overreacted to an unpleasant event, there is still much to be gained from the experience. Analyze what happened, using the procedure we've presented. Try to identify the self-talk at point B that caused your emotional upset at point C. Then think of ways to dispute your nonconstructive self-talk. Next time when that event or a similar one happens, you will be better able to cope with it constructively.

Also, keep in mind that nobody is happy, content, and calm all or even most of the time. The goal of this method is *not* to help you be some kind of robot who responds calmly and with little emotion to negative, unpleasant events. Being human, you are going to continue to feel hurt, disappointed, angry, or sad when some kinds of events occur, just as you are likely to feel pleased and happy when pleasant events occur. We hope that by using this method, you will be able to keep feelings of disappointment, anger, hurt, and upset at a more manageable level so that you can deal with life's difficulties and problems more constructively.

SUMMARY

This chapter presents a strategy for changing how you think about unpleasant, difficult situations so that you will be less upset by them and, therefore, able to deal with them more constructively. The basic idea of this approach is that it's *not* the unpleasant events that cause us to feel excessively bad or upset; rather, it's how we interpret or what we say to ourselves about the events that leads to our emotional overreaction.

We presented the A-B-C Method as a way for you to learn to identify your nonconstructive self-talk, and then suggested some guidelines for you to use in actively disputing and changing what you say to yourself when unpleasant situations occur.

REVIEW

☐ I understand how what I say to myself about difficult or unpleasant situations can lead to my emotional overreaction.

☐ I have learned to identify my nonconstructive self-talk about difficult or unpleasant events.

☐ I have begun actively disputing my nonconstructive self-talk by challenging the following:
   ☐ My highly evaluative ("should" and "ought") statements.
   ☐ My catastrophizing ("awful" and "terrible") statements.
   ☐ My overgeneralizations ("always" and "never" statements).

☐ I have been completing the self-monitoring form (Figure 10–1) each day.
   ☐ For the first week, I chose one unpleasant event and identified the activating event (A), the emotional consequences I experienced (C), and then my beliefs or self-talk (B) about A, which led to C.

☐ After the first week, I began disputing my self-talk and recording how I did this (Section D).

11

Being Your Own Coach: Self-Instructional Techniques

Kevin was a fast learner. He could understand how to use the techniques we presented to him and could give examples of how they might be used in a real-life situation. Thus, it was difficult to understand why he did not appear to be making much progress.

On questioning him carefully, we found that, although he understood what he wanted to do, he had a hard time thinking of it when the opportunity to try it presented itself. He was a good planner and a good hindsight critic, but when it came to implementing a course of action, he totally forgot all his plans.

What Kevin needed was someone at his side, reminding him of his well-laid plans. And that is exactly what he was able to get by learning how to be his own coach. What Kevin learned was how to give himself instructions at strategic times; that is, how to use what he had already learned in his day-to-day life. The kinds of techniques he learned are described in this chapter. They are useful when you know what you want to do but have a hard time doing it.

Many people who "know better" engage in behavior that either gets them into trouble or does not help them deal with difficult situations. Yet, they are able to point out what they could do to handle things in a more constructive way and may be able to give good advice to others.

The question we can ask ourselves, then, is how we can make the knowledge we have work for us when it counts. This chapter deals with one technique called *self-instruction;* that is, talking to yourself. This technique is neither childish nor crazy. It can be an effective way of helping you do what you plan to do. Everyone talks to himself to some extent, although one notices it only during fairly complex activities. For example, if you have to drive to a certain destination, you may find yourself carrying on a conversation in your head such as the following:

> Need to take the freeway exit from Watt Avenue South. Ahh, here it is. Now to Folsom in the middle lane so that I can be on the extreme right lane after I turn left. Then right at the light. There should be some railroad tracks. Good. Must be on the correct street. Left at the stop sign. Then right at the light and down one block.

Of course, the conversation may be less grammatically correct. It probably sounds like:

> Watt South? Middle Lane. Folsom? Left. Stop light? Good. Right turn. Tracks? Yep. Stop sign. Left. Light. Right. Good. Phew! Made it! On time? Hope so. . . .

This internal dialogue sounds very similar to one you might engage in if a friend were with you, giving you directions. In effect, you are silently talking with yourself. In this case, you are doing so in order to keep from getting lost—in order to get where you want to go. When used appropriately, self-talk helps us guide our behavior, gives us a sense of direction, and keeps us on track. It does this by making our goals concrete, by focusing our attention on the situation at hand, and by activating our memory so that we remember what our chosen plan of action is.

Another reason for the success of self-instruction is its distancing effect. You may have noticed that it is much easier to give advice to someone else in a tough situation than it is to think of it yourself when you are in similar straits. This is partly because one can be more objective and see a bigger picture when one is at a distance—psychologically as well as physically. You can create a beneficial distance by instructing yourself as you would instruct a friend. Imagine yourself trying to coach someone in your situation, and you will almost immediately get some perspective. By planning ahead, you can be prepared to coach yourself. By having a game plan, you'll be less likely to freeze when the moment comes.

If you have tried self-change programs before and haven't kept them up, or if you know what would get you out of your depression but you just haven't gotten around to do it, self-talk may be a useful skill for you to use systematically.

Self-talk helps you cope with situations in your daily life by helping you to do the following:

1. *Anticipating* what you want to accomplish in a given situation ("I want to chat with Lawrence after the sermon"); what the situation is going to be like ("There will be a lot of people milling around"); how you plan to handle it ("I will have to catch him early"); and exactly what you will do ("I will ask him about his job").
2. Keeping you *on track* and calm during the actual situation ("There are more people here than I expected, but I still want to talk with him. I've got to keep cool, and do what I planned anyway").
3. Helping you *handle good or bad situations* ("I am glad I talked to him. He is really nice," or "He was kind of nasty. Wonder what's bugging him?").
4. *Motivating* you to continue doing something you know will benefit you. ("I don't feel like putting in the energy to get out of this depressive pattern I'm in, but I know that once I get going, I'll feel better. Why punish myself by continuing to feel down?")

Examples of Self-Instruction

BAD-MEMORY BILL

One of the things that upset Bill the most was his bad memory. As he began to change his depressive behavior, he decided to work on his memory, too. (A book we have found helpful in this area is *The Memory Book* by Harry Lorrayne and Jerry Lucas.*) Bill liked many of the ideas in the book but found that he neglected to put them into practice. So he wrote out a set of directions for himself which he practiced and finally used to instruct himself: "OK. This is something I want to remember. I must make a ridiculous mental image of it and combine it with another such image so that one will bring up the other. Because I want to pick up typewriter ribbon before coming home, I'll imagine that I won't be able to get into the bus this afternoon because it is wrapped up with typewriter ribbon from a giant typewriter. The idea of not being able to get on the bus will trigger the image and remind me of the ribbon."

Bill found that telling himself what to do helped him to do it. And when he found himself feeling discouraged about his bad memory, he began to reassure himself as if he were talking to a friend: "As one gets older, some memory loss is normal. As long as you find a way around that, such as by using the memory skills you are learning, it won't become a nuisance. The more upset you get, the more grief you pile up on yourself. And getting upset about it doesn't help your memory a bit."

Bill found, in fact, that the more upset he became, the harder it was to remember things. By concentrating on his memory training and not allowing every minor instance of forgetting something to rattle him, he was able to feel better about himself and throw off one more obstacle to getting rid of his feelings of depression.

---

*H. Lorrayne and J. Lucas, *The Memory Book* (Briarcliff Manor, N.Y.: Stein & Day, 1974).

HIGH-EXPECTATIONS HANK

Like many other depressed people, Hank felt that he had never accomplished much. Yet, by any objective measure, Hank was clearly a competent person. The trouble was that Hank expected to be one of the best in a number of areas, and because he placed his goals at the highest possible levels, he couldn't always reach them. On top of that, he took for granted his accomplishments but was regularly miserable when he failed to do as well as he expected he should do.

Talking to Hank about lowering his expectations was futile. He had an answer for every argument we could bring up. So it was decided to have him work on himself. And, as usual, he did a good job:

"I know that having high goals helps me do my best and that I don't know if a goal is truly *unrealistic* until I try, but the fact that I am periodically disappointed enough to feel seriously depressed may indicate that I am setting self-expectations too high. Maybe instead of always comparing myself to the best in my field, I could sometimes compare myself to the average. Then I would come out looking good. Or, I could just notice the things I have done and not compare them to my goals or anyone else's goals. Setting high goals wouldn't be so bad if I also paid attention to medium ones."

In this case, consciously talking to himself helped Hank work through a very important issue. He continued to use self-instruction by periodically asking himself whether he had any "medium" goals at present, and by reminding himself that getting depressed over a disappointment was a waste of time and energy.

"REALISTIC" RACHEL

After reading each of the chapters which give instructions on how to break the depressive cycle, Rachel felt that they were unrealistic. "If things are lousy, why should I do something pleasant, or be sociable, or think positive thoughts? That wouldn't be honest or realistic; that would be just putting on an act, faking it. I'd just feel more depressed about lying to myself."

Rachel knew these techniques could help her control her depression, but she needed to convince herself to use them. She finally latched on to the distinction between constructive and destructive alternatives and began to instruct herself to look for the constructive ones.

A *constructive alternative* is one that helps you "put yourself together." Rachel found this distinction helpful and "realistic" when she remembered that a song she liked could make her feel really happy at times and really sad at other times. Because it was the same song, the happiness or sadness must be coming from her, not directly from the song.

Rachel's self-instructions began like this: "I know I am feeling depressed, and I know that when people feel depressed their reality is distorted in negative directions. Because that's the case with me, I need to balance things out by emphasizing constructive perspectives in my view of reality. What's the best way I could interpret what is happening right now?"

When her earlier doubts got in the way of her self-change efforts, she instructed herself to set them aside and consciously directed herself to continue with her plans and give them a proper test.

As soon as she overcame her depression, it was the negative, destructive perspectives she had once defended that seemed unrealistic to her.

Using Self-Instruction

Receiving instructions from someone else is most helpful when the instructor knows what he or she is talking about. Getting instructions on how to fix your auto from a brain surgeon who has never looked under the hood of a car would be a futile exercise. Similarly, giving yourself instructions works best when *you* know what *you* are talking about.

1. Understand what you want to accomplish. Be specific. Stating "I don't want to be depressed" is much too general.

Good: "I want to stop thinking in a depressed way."

Better: "I want to think in a less pessimistic manner."

Better still: "I want to remind myself 10 times each day that I *can* change the way I feel."

2. Understand how you plan to accomplish it. Be specific. Stating "I'll make an effort to remind myself" is too general.

Good: I'll reward myself for thinking that I *can* change how I feel."

Better: Each time I think to myself that I *can* change how I feel, I'll reward myself."

Better still: "Immediately after I think that I *can* change how I feel, I'll place a dime from my change purse into my left pocket. All the dimes I earn are mine to spend as I please.

Excellent: "Immediately after I think that I *can* change how I feel, I'll place a dime from my change purse into my left pocket. I'll place 10 dimes in my purse each morning, which means I can earn a dollar each day by thinking it 10 times, not less than 15 minutes apart. With the money I get each week, I can buy myself one of the following items: a table game, a record album, a book, an art print, a photography book, or a glider ride (which may take more than one week)."

3. Write down your instructions. It is easier to use self-instructions after you have written them down. Writing forces you to come up with *exact* words. This way you won't just *think* you know them—you'll see exactly what you know and what you are uncertain about.

4. Practice using the instructions. There are three good ways to practice:

Do It: Go through the process you have targeted and instruct yourself as planned. For example, if you have a hard time increasing positive thoughts and you have decided to tell yourself a positive thought before you eat anything during the day, tell yourself: "OK, before I take the first bite, I need to think one positive thought." Then think the positive thought, and take that first bite.

Imagine Doing It: Imagine instructing yourself during an important situation. For example, if you want to practice disputing your irrational ideas, think about a typical situation in which you are prone to let other people's remarks trigger depressive reactions in you. Then, imagine the whole scene, just as if you were seeing it on film. Listen to the spoken remarks that usually depress you. Then imagine instructing yourself: "OK, this is something that always gets to me. What am I telling myself to make myself depressed? How can I dispute that belief?" Actually pick out the irrational belief and dispute it on the spot. Replay the scene until you feel that you have handled it comfortably.

Imagine Someone Else Doing It: Pick someone who, in your opinion, satisfactorily handles situations you find difficult. Then use this person as a model. Again, imagine a whole scene, but this time it's not you but your chosen model who is starring. The model could be a friend, acquaintance, public figure, movie star, or a character from a book you've read. As the scene progresses, try to read your model's mind. What kind of self-instructions are going through his or her mind? For example, is he or she thinking: "I'll never get out of this mess, I just can't handle it. I'm just no good. I might as well give up"? *Or* "How can I get out of this mess? Let's see. Relax. Think clearly. If I do this, what will happen . . . ?" In other words, is the self-talk your model engages in destructive or constructive? Is it filled with hopelessness or optimism? Does it contain negatives or positives?

You can practice by placing your chosen model (or different models) in many situations in which *you* want to feel comfortable.

5. Modify your self-instructions. As you practice, you may realize that there are better self-instructions than the ones you came up with at first. Feel free to change them until you feel comfortable with them.

6. Build self-instructions into a routine. As soon as you begin to feel depressed, begin using self-instructions. You might tell yourself: "Is this something I want to think about right now? Do I want to save it for my worrying time or deal with it right now? What haven't I been considering lately? Have I been keeping up my pleasant activities? My social activities? My positive thoughts?" Once you have decided how you want to handle this particular feeling, coach yourself while you go about implementing your plan.

7. Reward yourself for using self-instructions.

SUMMARY

1. Self-instructions help you to do the following:

   –Remind yourself to do what you had planned.
   –Keep your task in focus
   –Motivate yourself in tough situations.
   –Maintain some beneficial psychological distance.

2. In order to learn to use self-instructions, you should do the following:

   –Understand *what* you want to do.
   –Understand *how* you want to do it.
   –Write down your instructions word for word.
   –Practice by doing it, by imagining yourself doing it, or by imagining a "model" doing it.
   –Modify your instructions as needed.
   –Build them into your daily routine.
   –Reward yourself for using them.

REVIEW

☐ I have read and understood what "self-instructions" are.

☐ I have read and understood the examples of people who have used self-instructions.

☐ I have decided not to try this technique at this time. (If you check this, skip the rest of the items and go to another chapter.)

☐ I have decided to try this technique.

☐ I have written down *what* I want to accomplish.

☐ I have written down *how* (specifically) I want to accomplish it.

☐ I have written down my self-instructions.

☐ I have practiced using self-instructions by:
   _____Doing it.
   _____Imagining, that I am doing it.
   _____Imagining someone else doing it.

☐ I have modified my self-instructions at least once.

☐ I have noticed myself using self-instructions spontaneously.

☐ I reward myself when I use self-instructions.

☐ I have used self-instructions to help myself practice techniques from Chapters _____, _____, and _____.

☐ I have kept track of my mood to see how using self-instructions influences it.

part three
LOOKING TOWARD THE FUTURE

12

Maintaining Your Gains

Let's get a reading on what you have done so far. By now you have made progress on several important goals. To help you assess your progress toward each goal, we will list them. Place a check mark in front of statements to which your answer would be "yes."

☐ Most importantly, *you* have been able to greatly reduce your depression level. To help you determine the truth of this statement, you should now fill out the Beck Depression Inventory again (using the copy at the back of this book) and compute your new score. At least one month should have passed since you first took this inventory.

My score on _____ (date) was _____.

My score today _____ (date) is _____.

☐ You have become more knowledgeable about the key symptoms of depression.

☐ You have become more sensitive in being able to recognize depression in yourself.

☐ You have gained a better understanding of what generally causes people to feel depressed.

☐ You have obtained knowledge about the kinds of situations, behaviors, and thoughts that contribute to your feeling depressed.

☐ You have learned how to design and how to carry out a self-change plan.

☐ You have been able to put this skill to work for you (Chapters 5, 6, 7, 8, 9, 10, 11). By changing your behavior and your life situations, you have been able to check your depression.

The remainder of this chapter is designed to accomplish the following:

1. To assist you in using what you have learned.
2. To encourage you to watch your depression level periodically so that you can recognize symptoms quickly.
3. To alert you to certain stressful events in life that often cause depression.

177

Integration

In this section we will briefly review Chapters 5 through 11 in order to personalize their content for you. The goal is to heighten your awareness of the kinds of behaviors and situations that lead to your feeling depressed. You can do this by assigning an importance rating to each of the statements in Table 12–1. Assign an importance rating of 2 if the statement has a high degree of relevance to your becoming depressed, a rating of 1 if it is somewhat important, and a rating of 0 if it is not relevant to you. After you record your importance ratings, you should also briefly describe the technique(s) you have found most useful for relevant problems.

Example: You know that you feel tense and anxious in many situations. This hinders your performance in those situations and makes you feel discouraged and dissatisfied with yourself. You would then give an importance rating of 2 to Statement 3 in Table 12–1. You have found that by practicing relaxation for 10 minutes before breakfast every day *and* before you encounter specific problem situations, you can avoid feeling tense and also reduce the frequency of your headaches. In the space provided you would indicate your technique for coping with a particular problem: (1) Practice relaxation 10 minutes before breakfast; (2) Relax for 3 minutes before (a) social gatherings, (b) business meetings, (c) giving a presentation before a group.

    Assigning importance to your problems and describing your methods of dealing with them will alert you to methods which you may want to repeat if you feel yourself becoming depressed again. Remember, an ounce of prevention is better, easier, and much less painful than a pound of treatment.

    In case you feel yourself becoming depressed again, focus on those problems you have judged to be of greatest importance to you. Put back into practice the techniques you have found most useful. Do you still have your self-change plans? Could you use them again? On the basis of your experience with them, are there changes you would want to make? If so, note these changes now.

TABLE 12–1

Statement	Priority Rating	Useful Technique(s)

Chapter 5, *Learning to Relax*
   I may become depressed when:
  1. I feel tense and upset a lot of the time.		

2. Feeling tense and anxious causes me to sleep poorly, to have headaches, and to feel tired.

3. I feel tense in specific situations, which

   a. Interferes with my performance in, and with my enjoyment of, these situations.

   b. Makes it difficult for me to participate in situations and to be as active as I would like to be.

Chapter 6, *Pleasant Activities*
I may become depressed when:

4. I allow my rate of pleasant activities to drop below a certain level.

   Estimate the daily number of pleasant activities needed to allow you to feel good.

   List those pleasant activities (aim for 10) that are especially important (good) for you.

5. I am unable to control my time so as to allow me to achieve a balance between what I must do and what I really want to do.

Chapter 7, *Learning How to Be Socially Skillful,* and Chapter 8, *Using Your Social Skills*
I may become depressed when:

6. My rate of social interactions and comfort drops below a certain level.

   What relationships and interactions do you see as most important to your well being? What problems do you see as still existing, or as potentially arising in the future, in these relationships?

   Is there anything you can do to anticipate, avoid, or cope with these problems?

7. I encounter social situations in which I feel rejected, disliked, and inferior.

8. I encounter situations in which I find it difficult to be appropriately assertive.

9. My interpersonal behavior becomes aversive to others, and, therefore, I am not being rewarded for my interactions.

Chapter 9, *Controlling Thoughts*
I may become depressed when:

10. I fail to generate enough positive thoughts about myself.

11. I generate a larger than average number of negative thoughts about myself.

TABLE 12–1 *(cont.)*

Statement	Priority Rating	Useful Technique(s)
Chapter 10, *Constructive Thinking*		
I may become depressed when:		
12. I overreact emotionally to situations because of what I tell myself about problems and difficulties.		
Chapter 11, *Self-Instructional Techniques*		
13. I fail to anticipate what I want to do and lose the chance to do it.		
14. I plan what I want to do but don't follow through when the time comes.		

Regular and Periodic Reassessment

There is complete agreement among the experts (a rare event!) that perventive measures are superior to treatment and that mild forms of any disorder are more easily helped than more severe and advanced forms. The key ideas are *prevention* and *early recognition.* Since you already know what it is like, we don't need to convince you that it is painful to be depressed. It is something that you want to avoid if you possibly can. Furthermore, depression often has a destructive impact on your immediate family as well as a negative effect on your own life. You also probably know from your own experiences that it is much easier to work yourself out of a mild depression than a more severe one. Nevertheless, it is hard for people to think preventively. Typically, we pay attention to our state of well-being only after something is drastically wrong. *It will take an active and conscious effort on your part to be alert to recurrences of depression.* You have an advantage over most people because you have learned how to recognize your own depression.

After you have stopped using this book regularly (we hope the reason is because you are not depressed any longer), we urge you to evaluate your depression level from time to time by filling out the Beck Depression Inventory (extra copies may be made from the form at the end of this book). Do this *regularly.* To do anything regularly, we need something to remind us. So, if you are going to evaluate yourself on a monthly basis (which is a fine idea), you might want to do it on payday (assuming that you get paid on a monthly basis). You could use any other "cue" which comes at regular monthly intervals. For example, you could use the arrival of your utility bill as a reminder. If you find that you are becoming more depressed, you should go back to *consistently* using the particular techniques you have found useful; *or*, if your situation has changed, you should go back to Chapter 4 to decide whether some other technique might be more useful to you.

Major Life Events and Life Changes That Often Cause Depression

A great deal has been learned in the past few years about the impact of stress on health in general and on mental health in particular. Stressful life events such as losing your job or learning that someone close to you is ill have a strong impact when they occur, making it much more likely that we will develop physical as well as mental problems, including depression. Depression is an especially common reaction to stressful life events like the death of loved ones and other separations (for example, children leaving home to get married or to go to college, accepting a job in a different part of the country, having close friends or relatives move away, or getting separated or divorced from one's spouse).

It is easy to understand why stressful life events that happen to us affect us to the great extent that they do. The often seriously disrupt and sometimes permanently change the pattern of our interactions and our life-style. A somewhat more subtle impact is how we are affected by stressful life events that happen to *other* people. We and the people with whom we interact are all part of a social family, and anything that affects one member of the "family" is likely to affect the other members as well. Thus, if your husband's mother dies, your husband is likely to feel depressed, be more withdrawn, and be less interested in you; this, in turn, will have an effect on *you*. Stressful life events of all kinds are likely to cause depression and require minor or major readjustments on each person's part. Table 12–2 lists events that may cause depression.

TABLE 12–2

List of Life Events That May Cause Depression

A. Social Separations
   1. Death of spouse, close family member, or close friend
   2. Divorce
   3. Marital separation
   4. Son or daughter leaving home
   5. Change in residence
B. Health-Related Events
   1. Major change in health of self or close family member
   2. Personal injury or illness

TABLE 12–2

List of Life Events That May Cause Depression

C. New Responsibilities and Adjustments
 1. Marriage
 2. Addition of new family member
D. Work-Related Events
 1. Change to different jobs
 2. Promotion and/or major change in work responsibilities
 3. Being fired
 4. Trouble with boss
 5. Retirement from work
 6. Spouse starts or stops work
 7. Change to new school
 8. End of formal schooling
E. Financial and Material Events
 1. Burdensome debts
 2. Financial setbacks
 3. Loss of personal property through fire, theft, etc.
 4. Legal problems

Prepare and Plan for Stressful Life Events

Many stressful life events are predictable and can be anticipated. You usually know ahead of time that your child will go to college, will get married, or will move out of your home; that your close friend or someone in your family is going to move; that your spouse is going to retire (or you are); that a cold and dreary winter is approaching; that you and your spouse will separate; that you are going to lose your job; or that your spouse will have to go to the hospital for an operation.

You can prepare for stressful life events in three ways:

1. Carefully anticipate the specific ways in which the stressful life event will affect your life and your activities. Separations (permanent or temporary) from people with whom you have been closely involved are likely to leave a big *void* in your life. Many of your activities with that person, which may have been a major part of your life, will no longer occur.

2. Prepare for stressful events by developing a self-change plan. Make use of the skills you have acquired in the previous chapters to deal with the problem(s) the event will create for you.

3. Monitor or evaluate your depression level more closely. If you find yourself becoming more depressed, put back into practice some of the techniques that you have found useful.

Unfortunately, some stressful life events occur unexpectedly—often when we are least likely to expect them. We cannot prepare for such unexpected events, but we *can* plan to cope with them after they have happened. A physically disabling disease or accident may make it impossible for us to engage in many of the activities we were accustomed to doing. A stroke may leave a person with impairments in his or her ability to communicate, an obviously very important skill in social interactions. Many serious health conditions drastically limit our ability to move, impair our coordination, and lower our energy level. All of these are stressful life events that seriously interfere with our ability to do pleasant activities. These events are, therefore, likely to lead to depression. By recognizing specific problems, a self-change plan can be developed to avoid, or at least to minimize, the resulting feeling of depression.

Stress (and, hence, depression) may also be associated with positive events that require change and new adjustments and are important aspects of our life style. These include the following:

1. Graduating from school: Deadlines, time schedules, exams, grades, fear of failure, pride of being in a particular program or class, and other factors that have acted to motivate the person and to organize his or her time are lost.

2. Promotions: Getting "kicked upstairs" is likely to interrupt existing relationships; buddies become subordinates, and the quality of the relationships is likely to be affected. The usual work with which the person felt comfortable and pleased is replaced by new assignments with uncertain outcomes.

3. Getting married: This change presents a host of new responsibilities and adjustments to day-to-day living.

4. Addition of a child, or anyone else, to the household: This type of change places additional demands on one's time and may drastically affect one's marital relationship.

5. Change in residence: This change disrupts a person's ongoing relationships and many other activities; it requires a person to develop a new set of friendships and relationships.

6. Changes in life-style of spouse (for example, one's spouse goes back to school, takes a job after years of being a housewife, or retires): This situation introduces major changes in the activities a couple engages in and affects the amount of time a couple spends together.

The key idea is to be alert to the possible impact *on you* from the life event. The questions to ask are the following:

1. *Specifically* how will the event effect my life? Will it result in my having a lot of time on my hands? Will it separate me from people with whom I have been close and with whom I have enjoyed interacting? Will it make it more difficult for me to do many of the activities I like to do? Will it change the behavior of other people toward me?

2. Is the event likely to cause me to feel depressed?

3. What can I do to prepare for, and to cope with, the changes in the pattern of my interactions that will be brought about by the event? (The priority ratings you assigned to the behaviors and situations that lead to your feeling depressed in Table 12–1 and the techniques you have found most useful for controlling your depression may be useful guides for the design of a self-change program to deal with the problems the event will create for you.)

REVIEW

☐ I have reevaluated my depression level by taking the Beck Depression Inventory again.

☐ I have a pretty clear idea of what types of conditions are associated with my feeling depressed, and I have listed the techniques I found useful for controlling my depression.

☐ I will assess my depression level with the Beck Depression Inventory at regular intervals (preferably once a month).

☐ I understand the importance of being especially alert to the occurrence of stressful life events and life changes that might happen to me or people who are part of my "social network."

☐ I understand the importance of actively coping with life events by noting how they will affect my life pattern and by developing a self-change plan to cope with the problems that certain events will create for me.

13

Changing Your Personality

We believe that people can change. Some people argue that our personalities are permanently formed after the early years of life and that change thereafter is very difficult, if not impossible. We don't agree. As long as you are alive, you will be growing and changing. Human beings are the most adaptable and flexible form of life on earth. If you try to plant your feet too firmly in one spot, you may slow down change, but you will also be giving up one of your most precious human abilities.

You may have already changed a great deal from working on this book. However, you should not feel that your changes are over! As long as you live, you will need to keep changing and adapting—as the world around you changes, as your own body changes, and as your friends and loved ones change. We are different at age 40 from how we were at 20 or will be at 70.

The issue of this chapter is not what specific changes you want to make, but a larger question: *Who are you and who might you become?* Seeing change and growth as lifelong processes is important; change is a part of your rich human capacity. This chapter will help you plan in what direction your changes should head. Since people often have objections and fears when they consider making changes, this chapter will begin by spelling out some of the most common fears, and what we hope will be convincing arguments for why each fear should be abandoned. The chapter will then address the questions of how you create yourself by the choices you make and how to plan changes that will shape and define much of your life.

Common Fears about Changing

FEAR OF LOSING THE STATUS QUO

Some people feel safety in stability even if they are unhappy about their current situation. The situation may not be good, but at least it is familiar. Noticing change in ourselves or in people close to us can be threatening because it means there may be new dangers ahead. Also, being aware of change means becoming aware of the fact that we, and other people, are inevitably getting older. This is an easy fear to understand because, to some extent, we all share it. However, it is not a good reason to avoid thinking about change. The fear is based on the recognition that change comes to us all and change brings unfamiliar experiences. But this will happen, whether we like it or not. It is much better to plan for change and accept it than to pretend you can prevent it! You can learn to anticipate change not as a danger but as an opportunity to plan new and positive life experiences.

FEAR OF INCONSISTENCY

Sometimes people are afraid to change because they do not want to appear to be fickle or inconsistent. They fear that behaving in a new way will "cheapen" their self-image or that others will consider them "two-faced." Such a view implies that most people behave in a very consistent manner and, thus, that consistency is "normal." However, psychologists now know that, in fact, most of us are not extremely consistent. Flexibility seems to be the rule rather than rigid consistency; people's behavior tends to change to fit the situation. For example, you may be very friendly at a neighborhood gathering but very stiff and formal at a fancy restaurant. Similarly, you may be very meticulous and careful in your work but carefree and happy-go-lucky on weekends.

Ralph Waldo Emerson, an early American writer and philosopher, wrote about human adaptability before psychologists began to understand it. He said, "A foolish consistency is the hobgoblin of little minds." Those who fear adaptive change are limiting themselves, and they will lead small lives—and, we might add, unhappy lives as well.

FEAR THAT CHANGE
IS AN ADMISSION OF FAILURE

Sometimes people are afraid to change because they think other persons would interpret change as an admission of personal failure. This is a destructive attitude, and it also implies a very negative view of human adaptability. Our feeling about this is different. We believe that all people do the best they can at any given time; you are doing the best you can now, given such things as what you know, where you live, and what help you get from other people. But that doesn't mean that you will always want to do just what you are doing now. You may want to be different; you may be able to solve some life problems better at a later time; or you may just feel that it's time for a change. Changing simply means that you are adapting, either because you know something now that you didn't before or because your world changed. Dinosaurs remained the same when their world changed, and then they became extinct. Change would have been a success for the dinosaurs: *lack* of change is often the *real* failure. You are a human, blessed with great adaptability. For you, too, change can be a great success rather than a sign of failure.

FEAR OF LOSING SPONTANEITY

Sometimes people resist change because they feel that life should just flow naturally, without any conscious effort or careful planning. However, in reality that goal is seldom, if ever, achieved. All of us *create ourselves each day* by choosing to behave in certain ways. Our choices are not completely "free." They are certainly influenced by the environment we inhabit, the consequences of our choices, and the behavior of our peers. However, as humans we can *consider* a great deal of information— including all these factors and more—in making choices. Often you do this so spontaneously or automatically that you are hardly aware of the activity of choosing; for instance, you probably get up and begin your daily work without thinking about the fact that you are making a *choice* about how to spend the day. At other times, decisions may seem painfully conscious. Whether your choices are simple or complex, you make them all the time, and you can always make new ones. Humans become spontaneous and natural by choosing well and wisely, not by refusing to make any choices at all (which is, after all, a choice in itself).

FEAR OF EXPERIMENTING

Change is risky; we never know ahead of time just what a change will bring. Sometimes, we just might make things worse; that is a real risk. Other changes may work out very well, but you will never know ahead of time which changes will work and which will not. The important thing to remember is to stay flexible and to be sensitive to what is happening. That way, if things don't work out, you can back off and try something else. By taking a risk now and then, you are able to improve your life in the long run. George Kelly, a noted psychologist, was fond of using science as an example. Each of us, just like the scientist, must continually experiment in our lives, trying out possibilities and learning from what works and what doesn't work. Refusing to experiment is, in the long run, much more risky and limiting.

Creating Yourself

WHO YOU MIGHT BE

Being eager to experience change is only one step along the road, although it is a very crucial one. The next step is knowing what kinds of changes you want and how to go about creating them.

One of the first important things for you to realize is that there is no *one* way to create a good life. Unhappy people sometimes think there is a "secret to life" that would unlock happiness if it were only known. But there is no secret; life is very complex and we all have to find our own way—primarily by helping to create it. We shall highlight that complexity by describing a few people. The purpose of these brief sketches is to demonstrate that a successful life can be fashioned in a number of ways.

"Susie"—This sketch describes a woman in her mid-50s who has a successful business career:

> Susie is an extremely competent person. She knows what she wants and she usually knows how to accomplish what she plans. People like and respect Susie because they can count on her; if she makes a promise, she keeps it.
>
> Susie is not always easy to get to know, partly because she is a busy person. In addition, because she is bright and active people are sometimes reluctant to discuss personal things with her. Consequently, Susie has a few very close friends who really understand her, but a large number of casual acquaintances with whom she has worked at one time or another.
>
> Susie is happy and successful because she uses her intelligence wisely both at work and in her personal relationships.

"Sharon"—This sketch describes a young woman who has just begun working after completing high school. She hopes to marry and has no particular career plans.

> Sharon is a gentle person. People like her because she is willing to take time to help them; she always has a kind word to say. She speaks softly and listens a lot. At parties, she usually talks to one person at a time instead of being part of a noisy group. When Sharon gets upset about something, she usually turns to her closest friends for support. She's not afraid to share her feelings with them because she trusts their feelings for her. They are glad to help her, because she can always be counted on to help other people.

"Sam"—This sketch describes a man in his early 40s. He has a good job and makes a good salary; he does not expect or desire much advancement in his company.

Sam is extremely self-confident and attractive. He uses these attributes well and without arrogance. He enjoys his life, is able to make friends easily, and expects to be able to do most things he would like to do. People say he has an easy, graceful manner that is enjoyable. Sam is not a great conversationalist, nor does he have major life goals and plans. Instead, he relies on his abilities and trusts that things will continue to work out for him.

Sam is happy and successful because he has self-confidence, which is based on an honest assessment of his talents. He allows his natural talents free rein, but does not think that he is better than other people because of the skills he possesses.

"Joe"—This sketch describes a 20-year-old college student. He majors in elementary education and plans to become a teacher.

Joe is an extrovert. He is outgoing, cheerful, and full of energy; as a result, he's usually the one to organize events among the people he knows. He likes fun; his projects are rarely "productive." Instead he focuses on physical activities, large parties, trips to the beach, and other group activities. At a party, he is usually either dancing or talking in a group.

Joe has lots of friends, and he is constantly making new ones. His relationships are not superficial; he honestly enjoys others and he shares himself openly. However, his relationships usually do not proceed to depth or intimacy, since there is little chance to sit and talk quietly with Joe.

Overall, Joe is happy because he has an active life and lots of friends, which he wants.

"Jerry"—This sketch describes a man in his late 60s who has been married to the same person for 40 years. He completed high school and two years of college; he retired two years ago.

Jerry is a happy man whose life now centers on his family. He is married and has two children and five grandchildren. These relationships are enormously important to him. He likes other people and has friends, but it is clear that home is his highest priority. His family loves him, partly because of his love and devotion to them, but they also love him because of his enthusiasm and eagerness to enjoy life. Jerry plans hikes and raft trips for the family; he maintains a garden and gives food to friends and neighbors as well as his family. He also reads and shares new ideas with the entire family.

After retiring, Jerry at first found that he had time on his hands, but after thinking about his priorities he was able to develop this new life-style. He has found it very rewarding, and wonders how he used to find time for work! Jerry is a happy person because he has been able to reexamine what he wants in life at this time, and he works hard at making that a success.

Creating Your Own Role Sketch

The examples presented here are diverse, but they all contain common elements: They all address what the person's goals are, what the person's style is like, and what the person's relationships are like. There are innumerable ways to work out these elements, but they *all* need to work in order for the overall picture to be complete. In this next section, try to create a role sketch for yourself.

There are two ways to go about this task. One is to reject your current personality and "start from scratch" by describing the person you really want to be. We do not believe that this way of proceeding is a very good idea. Instead, we recommend a second way of approaching the role sketch, which is to accept most of your current personality but to improve it by suggesting *modifications*. In this recommended approach, a role sketch should sound a lot like the person you are right now. If you are quiet and gentle like Sharon, don't write an "extrovert" profile like Joe's for yourself (unless you're willing to go through a long and very difficult process of change). Use the good qualities you already have as the core of a successful role sketch. Whichever approach you take, the role sketch should contain all the elements that we've mentioned: life goals, personal style, and nature of relationships. These should be well worked out in way that can succeed for you (not for your neighbor, or the person you were 10 years ago, or your "dream self"—they have to work for *you*).

Finally, the role sketch should describe the changes you will need to make to get from where you are now to where you want to be. How different from you is the successful, happy person you describe? If you've done the job as we recommend, the role sketch should be a lot like you, but it should have important, clearly definable differences from your current self-description. Those clearly definable differences will become the basis of your plans for change.

Here's a guide to help you put all this together. If you become confused, look back at the role sketches on the previous pages, and use them to give you ideas about how to get started. In addition, Figure 13–1 shows a role sketch about "Sandra," who was formerly depressed but has become much happier as a result of working on her problems. In particular, Sandra has increased her pleasant activities, learned to relax in social situations, and has changed some nonfunctional beliefs—for example, the belief that everyone must love her.

Sandra's role sketch is systematically structured to give you a guide in putting together your own sketch. Use the form shown in Figure 13–2 to write your own role sketch.

FIGURE 13–1
Role Sketch of Sandra

1. *My highest priorities* (life goals, major commitments, and so on)   My greatest commitment is to my marriage and my family. I also hope to use my professional training but would not sacrifice my family for it. I want to be cared for by those who mean the most to me, not necessarily by everyone.
2. *Personal style*   I am soft-spoken, gentle, and generous. I enjoy having fun with a small group; I don't like big parties. I like doing active things— playing games, sports, hikes—more than sitting around talking. I work hard, because I enjoy accomplishment and coming through for people.
3. *Relationships*   People don't get to know me easily, but once they do know me they like and trust me. I avoid relationships with people who "live for the moment." I like more intimate, long-lasting relationships.
4. *Summary: I can be happy and successful because*   I fit my goals and social activities to my quiet style, instead of trying to force myself to be more outgoing. I am likeable for my warm, hard-working, reliable style, and I can really accomplish my goals with those qualities.
5. In clearly specified ways, how is this person I hope to be different from my present self-description?

   I need to develop more of the giving warmth I describe here.
   I need to relax more at work and remember that I work to accomplish things, not to become famous and beloved.
   I've improved a lot in enjoying the company of others in small groups, but I could still work on this a little.

FIGURE 13–2
Role Sketch Form

1. My highest priorities (life goals, major commitments, and so on)

2. Personal style

3. Relationships

4. Summary: I can be happy and successful because

5. In clearly specified ways, how is this person I hope to be different from my present self-description?

Trying Out the Role

Now you are ready to try out some life changes. There are several things to keep in mind as you do this. First, this is just an experiment! You don't know for sure how these changes will work until you try them, so don't worry about failure. If this role doesn't work out, you can try out another one. You will gradually find one that's right for you if you keep trying and keep modifying and adapting. It may be helpful to tell yourself over and over that it is "only practice." You aren't in a tournament—you're just warming up and practicing a skill. If you don't do well, it just means you need a little more practice.

Second, remember to set realistic goals for yourself. You can't change your facial features by trying out a role sketch, nor can you become self-confident overnight. You are not trying to become a new person; you are just trying to be a happier, more adaptive, more flexible person than you were before.

Third, use and reuse this book to help you reach your goals. Remember what you have learned about using social learning principles to guide change. Try out chapters that didn't seem crucial before, particularly if your role sketch suggests that they would be helpful now. Keep doing the things that have helped you thus far while you make your new changes.

Looking at the Future

Throughout this chapter, we have suggested that life is a constant process of change; we have tried to show you how to change without fear about the directions you choose for yourself. It might be a good idea to plan to make this a lifelong process. At regular intervals—for instance, every year on your birthday—you might write out a role sketch for yourself using the format in this chapter.* Don't look at your previous role sketches until you have writen your current one. Then go back and compare who your are now with earlier role sketches. This will show vividly both how you have changed and how you have built on what came before. Change and continuity should both emerge, forming a pattern.

SUMMARY

This chapter has discussed the need for continual change in your life. Even if you have successfully overcome your depression, you will still need to change as you grow older and your life circumstances change. We

---

*Another copy of the Role Sketch Form is included in the section titled *Extra Forms*, beginning on page 211.

have discussed some fears that people report when they look ahead and consider the changes to come. We have tried to show that these fears are groundless and that you should embrace change, seeing it as an opportunity to experience new facets of life.

This chapter has also presented a brief method for thinking about what changes you need in order to become more like the person you really want to be. This role-sketch method can be used throughout your life to help you follow the patterns of change and continuity that you experience.

REVIEW

☐ I have written a role sketch for myself.

☐ I have figured out how to work on the changes I still have to make in order to be more like my role sketch. I will do the following:

    ☐ Use the following additional chapters in the book:_____
    _____.

    ☐ Keep working on some things I have started, using the following chapters:_____.

    ☐ Use another self-help book: _____.

    ☐ See a counselor.

    ☐ Other: _____.

☐ I will rewrite my role sketch at the following regular interval:
_____.

14

Planning Your Future

As we near the end of our book, we'd like to talk with you about what comes next. We have shared what we think are helpful ideas with you, and we hope these ideas will continue to have some influence in your life as the years go by. People often react to crises by putting new ideas into practice, but when the crises pass, they return to their old patterns. So we'd like to share these ideas with you:

1. Think preventively and in terms of positive mental health.
2. Planning is related to mental well-being.
3. Consider the high moments in your life, the "peak experiences." Learn to recognize them and make room for them.

Preventive Thinking and Beyond

Many people pay attention to their well-being only when it shows clear signs of deteriorating. They have a picture of "average" or "normal" health in their minds, and when they fall below this norm they run hard to catch up with it. Once they feel they have reached an "average" state of well-being, they again neglect the factors that can give them even greater strength. By continuing to plan one's daily life from a "positive health" perspective, one can nourish one's physical and psychological potential, thus increasing one's enjoyment of life and forestalling serious consequences if a serious energy-draining crisis occurs.

Psychological prevention is a much neglected area. There is so much need for giving services to people who are hurting that we do not take the time to prepare those people who are not hurting to live life in effective ways. If we did, we might be able to prevent many people from becoming casualties. The savings in therapy time and money—not to mention human suffering—could be enormous. Perhaps some day "psychological impact statements" will be as familiar to our ears as "environmental impact statements."

Much of the material in Chapter 12, *Maintaining Your Gains*, can serve as a preventive function in your life. Note, in particular, the section entitled *Major Life Events and Life Changes That Often Cause Depression*. But remember that the stress produced by change need *not* be destructive. If used well, these events can be beneficial to one's growth and fulfillment. By anticipating and preparing for them, we can increase the chances that we will be able to use them effectively.

Instead of waiting until we are left behind and then running hard to catch up, we can maintain a steady pace that conserves energy for the really hard places. This involves looking ahead, of course, and it turns out that doing so is in itself healthy. But that is the second idea we want to mention.

Planning and Mental Health

Recent research attempting to discover factors related to psychological adjustment has determined that those people rated as well-adjusted are good at (1) knowing the consequences of their acts, and (2) planning ahead to obtain their goals.

This is not surprising, of course. After all, it makes intuitive sense that aimlessness is likely to be accompanied by boredom and feelings of worthlessness. Having a goal, a direction, seems to get one's body and mind in tune and one's energy directed harmoniously toward its destination.

As you consider the years ahead, it would be worth your while to think about how your plans are going to harmonize your values with your goals. Let's start by defining the two terms *values* and *goals*.

Values are general principles or guidelines you consider desirable and worthwhile. *Goals* are specific ends toward which you direct your efforts. Hopefully, your goals will be compatible with your values; that is, your specific ends will follow from your general principles.

For example, if you have the protection of the environment as a value and the ownership of a large, high-powered automobile as a goal, you will have to do some thinking about how the two fit (or don't fit) together. You may decide that, to stay within your value system, you will have to buy one of the most gas-efficient cars available, and certainly not a big 8-cylinder gas-guzzler. Or, you may conclude that buying *any* kind of a car would go against your values, and instead decide to ride a bike to work.

If your value system includes enjoying the fruits of your labor as you see fit (and does not include environmental concerns), then you will not have to limit your search for a car in any way. If you have both sets of values, you probably will have to do some compromising or decide that one value has precedence over the other.

Note that your goal gets meaning and worth from your values. Even if you decide not to get a car, that decision has positive emotional tone when it stems from a clearly defined value. Compare it, for example, to not getting a car because you don't have the money. In both cases, you wind up with no car, but in the former case, you are likely to have a greater feeling of satisfaction than in the latter. Values (general guidelines) give meaning to goals (specific plans).

Sometimes values contradict each other. If you value a close-knit family and also value staying free of responsibility for others, one or the other value must change. In such cases, the most adaptive outcome will be to acknowledge both sets of values and choose between them or blend them into a realistic new value. In this case, for example, the new value might be an equalitarian family system in which everyone shares responsibility according to their age and capabilities. The goal for an individual with this value would probably be to find and attempt to become close to like-minded members of the opposite sex. Later, the goal would be to rear children who would become self-sufficient. Note that you would have to take on some responsibilities, but perhaps not as much as you originally feared. If you have to choose between the two values, at least you'll have the knowledge that you are giving up something for something even more desirable.

Another alternative, of course, would be to decide to abide by one value for a period of time and then focus on the other value. This is probably the most common choice in relation to rearing a family: being single, then being married with no children, and then having children. The length of each of these periods probably varies with the importance of independence or family ties for the individual.

The important point is that awareness of conscious choice between such values makes it less likely that one would destructively berate oneself for not having heeded whichever value necessarily gets lower priority. Values that we have found to cause considerable conflict among depressed persons include the following:

–Wanting to be a good mother and wife *and* wanting to have a career.
–Wanting to keep the family together *and* wanting a divorce.
–Wanting to have money in the bank *and* wanting to help one's child through college.
–Wanting to be very successful in one's line of work *and* wanting to spend more time with one's family.

These are not easy choices to make, but we do make them, even by default. If a choice is proving very hard for you and if the indecision is becoming a source of serious stress, we recommend visiting a professional counselor or other mental-health professional. He or she cannot make the decision *for* you, but a counselor can help you see things more clearly and give some support as you make a clear choice.

Another source of difficulty can spring up when we fail to achieve a certain goal and, as a result of frustration, we give up both the goal and the value behind it.

> Phil valued family life and hoped to marry someone who would share that dream with him. However, after he fell in love with a girl named Jean, Jean decided that she did not want to marry him. Phil proceeded to get involved in a number of brief relationships and claimed he was sure he would never get married. The unsatisfying, cynical flavor of these relationships finally convinced Phil that he was throwing out a *value* he still held when he gave up the *goal* of marrying Jean. Only then was he able to enter into relationships with an open mind and allow himself to entertain seriously the possibility of a permanent relationship.

If a value change occurs in a deliberate manner, then the person has made a conscious choice for which he or she is responsible. If, however, the value change occurs as an automatic reaction to frustration (as when it occurs "out of spite") or in a "sour grapes" manner, then the person is losing a certain amount of freedom. Our values *are* subject to some degree of choice, and in making this choice we determine, in large part, whether or not we will obtain self-fulfillment.

Values are influenced by our upbringing, our education, our readings, the mass media, and our social group. Values can be reinforced symbolically, through encouragement for their verbal or behavioral expression. We have a hand in determining which values will be most important in our lives by placing ourselves in situations in which certain values are reinforced. For example, by attending lectures, reading books, or associating with people who believe in specific values, we can strengthen those particular values.

Since this is the case, we can maintain our freedom of choice in regard to values and associated goals by *deliberately arranging social support systems* that will motivate us to continue on a road we have chosen and by avoiding energy-draining individuals or groups that punish our pursuit of cherished goals.

We have talked about values in an abstract way thus far. To help clarify our discussion, we will now list some of the many goals human beings have at their disposal. These goals can be individual or interpersonal, short-term or long-term, or superordinate goals.

INDIVIDUAL GOALS

These goals include:

1. Life-style (which involves choosing the kind of image one would like to fashion oneself into).
2. Spiritual, religious, or philosophical activities.
3. Economic pursuits.
4. Educational plans.
5. Vocational choices.
6. Physical activity level.
7. Recreational and creativity-oriented activities.

Note that in all of these areas there is no way to avoid making choices. For example, if you choose not to concern yourself with physical activity, you are probably choosing a low level of physical activity. The more aware you are of the many choices to be made, the less likely you are to merely drift into one of them.

INTERPERSONAL GOALS

These goals, by their very nature, involve interaction with others:

1. Family life-style: degree of closeness with parents, spouse, children, and other family members.
2. Friends: number of people, degree of intimacy, source (work, hobbies, geographic closeness, political similarities, and so on).
3. Romantic relationships: seriousness, sexual involvement, financial understandings, exclusiveness versus multiple relationships, equalitarian versus "traditional" styles, expectations regarding the future, and so on.
4. Group commitments: degree of involvement with social and community groups, time priorities for group activities versus personal or family activities, level of emotional dependence on groups.
5. Leadership roles: how much influence one wants to exercise on groups, how much responsibility one wants to undertake, how much recognition one wants to receive.

Take the time now to note briefly your present goals in each of these areas.

INDIVIDUAL GOALS

1. Life-style _____

2. Spiritual, religious, or philosophical activities _____

3. Economic pursuits _____

4. Educational plans _____

5. Vocational choices _____

6. Physical activity level _____

7. Recreational and creativity-oriented activities _____

INTERPERSONAL GOALS

1. Family life-style _____

2. Friends _____

3. Romantic relationships _____

4. Group commitments _____

5. Leadership roles _____

SHORT-TERM GOALS

These goals are the kind that can be placed on a "to do" list, such as meeting new people, completing a project, making an appointment, writing a letter, calling a friend, reading a book, and so on. These day-to-day goals are important because they have a great influence on one's daily mood shifts.

LONG-TERM GOALS

These goals help to place the short-term goals in perspective. They also help you come up with short-term goals that will increase your chances of reaching your long-term goals.

You may come up with your own long-term goals by looking at the "individual" and "interpersonal" goal lists and answering these two questions regarding each of the items:

1. Where would you like to be in regard to each of the items 10 years from now? 20 years from now? 30 years from now?
2. In looking back 10, 20, and 30 years from now, what kind of memories would you like to have about the present?

The first question should help you make plans for the future. The second question should help you make plans for now. Even though you may not have thought about it before, you can arrange to have pleasant memories in the future by engaging in satisfying activities now.

SUPERORDINATE GOALS

These are all-encompassing life goals. Some people find them to be very useful to give perspective to their present situations and to give direction to their lives.

These goals include "philosophies of life" or "reasons for living" such as religious commitments; political causes; humanitarian projects; struggles for economic security for oneself and one's heirs; aesthetic pursuits; thirst for knowledge, pleasure, fame, power, justice, or enlightenment; the desire to love and be loved; and the decision to be open to existence.

Being aware of these goals helps many people avoid aimless drifting. Superordinate goals help to provide order for the less inclusive goals mentioned earlier. They can be effective in getting people out of destructive ruts by organizing their energy and directing it toward a destination that they consider worthwhile.

Take a few moments now to jot down your "philosophy of life":

If I had to tell someone what life is all about for me, I would say:

_____

_____

_____

_____

_____

_____

_____

_____

_____

_____

_____

Do not read ahead until you take the time to fill out your philosophy of life. The following examples may bias your own ideas if you read them first. Put the book down now. Take some time to think about your life and then come back and jot it down.

My Philosophy of Life, by Ana, a 46-year-old housewife.

The most important things in my life are to be good to my family and faithful to my God. I believe that raising my children to respect other people as well as themselves and to learn to take good care of themselves in this world are some of the best things a mother can do. I also believe that means setting a good example by taking care of myself and my needs. That's why I always set aside time for me and my husband to enjoy times together by ourselves. I'd like to be known as an interesting, likable woman who is a good mother and a good wife.

My Philosophy of Life, by Gina, a 30-year-old lawyer.

I believe strongly in reaching the highest goals one can. My profession is my most important goal right now, and I'd like to dedicate myself to becoming well-known and respected in my field. I also believe that I should use my knowledge and energy to help bring about societal change by working within the system. Having good companionship is something that I guess I consider important, but I have not spent much energy on it for a while, and I don't really feel a need to do so at the present.

My Philosophy of Life, by Mark, a 36-year-old waiter.

I guess I see my life as a time for learning and experiencing many things. I really don't know if there is much life after death, and I don't spend much time thinking about it. I like to have time to travel, to eat good food, to meet and get close to many different women, to read, listen to music, and so on. I like having money in my pocket and spending it any way I want to. I like feeling healthy, so I take good care of my body. If I ever have kids, I'd like to teach them to enjoy life the way I have.

My Philosophy of Life, by Phil, a 26-year-old teacher.

My basic philosophy of life is to be responsible but not perfectionistic. The most important people in my life are my parents, my wife, and my kids. Next in line are my students. I believe that the most worthwhile thing a human being can do is learn about the world. To learn the most, one needs to learn to read and to think; that's what I try to teach my kids and my pupils. In order to have the luxury to learn, you have to be secure, so having enough money is really important to me. But, in a way, learning is still the most important because having enough money is really the result of having learned to earn it.

An essential element in planning involves learning to put your goals in priority order. This involves the ability to discriminate between more and less important goals as well as the ability to winnow out destructive goals. To help you get a start, we'll mention a few examples.

First, we consciously leave out destructive goals such as perfectionism, (which is unattainable) and the goal of considering oneself either "the best" or "a failure" (which is a common destroyer of many fine human beings). Note that we do *not* mean to condemn the goal of striving for excellence. We *do* condemn the practice of equating failure to be "perfect" or "the best" with "total failure" as a person.

Another common destructive goal is setting goals for other people and making *our* happiness dependent on *their* reaching the goals. This is most often seen in parents who place all their expectations of fulfillment on their children or in teachers who feel that they have failed if their students do not "make good" later in life.

Having screened out goals that we consider destructive, we can now begin to consider constructive goals. As an example, let's look at Abraham Maslow's hierarchy of motivators.[1] Maslow, a famous humanistic psychologist, spoke of *physiological needs*, such as need for food and water; *safety needs*, such as need for predictability and ways to cope with danger; *belongingness and love needs*, such as being part of a community and being emotionally important to others; *self-esteem needs*, such as feeling pride in one's characteristics and one's accomplishments; and the *need for self-actualization*, which involves going beyond survival needs and reaching the highest level of human functioning.

Whether or not you agree with this list of human priorities, it can serve as a model for putting together your own list. In particular, note that the list includes some goals we generally take for granted, such as having enough food to eat. Even if these goals are already being met, it may be worth your while to include them to increase your awareness of how much you are already accomplishing.

Recognizing and Appreciating "Peak Experiences"

This book deals with depression, a psychological state characterized by dysphoria. Thus far, we have showed you ways to bring this experience under control, returning your mood to normal levels. In this chapter, we have spoken about planning and prevention as ways to avoid experiencing deep depression in the future. But we have not addressed the other end of the mood spectrum, that is, the feeling of *euphoria*.

Webster's dictionary defines euphoria as "an often unaccountable feeling of well-being or elation." We think that by becoming aware of this experience when it occurs, you may learn to recognize the circumstances in which it is likely to come about. You may then learn to "set the stage" or facilitate its emergence.

To help you recognize this psychological state, we would like to use the descriptions Abraham Maslow collected from observing people talking about their happiest moments, ecstatic moments, and the most wonderful experiences of their lives. These are the moments Maslow calls "peak experiences."

Persons in the peak experience feel more integrated, more unified, and yet more able to fuse with the world. They feel that they are at the peak of their powers and have a sense of effortlessness and ease. They feel more self-determined, more responsible, and at the same time most free of inhibitions and fears. They are therefore more spontaneous and relaxed, and also more creative, novel, and fresh.

[1]Maslow, A. M., *Toward a Psychology of Being*, 2nd ed. (New York: Von Nostrand Reinhold, 1968).

During the peak experience, people feel unique, more purely different. They are "all there," more in the here-and-now than at other times. They feel less restricted by physical limitations, as though they were "pure psyche." They have a sense of non-striving and non-needing, and yet they deeply appreciate their situation, wanting to express their reactions to it in a poetic manner that blends easily with a feeling of playfulness, delight, and happy, childlike joy. This is accompanied by a sense of gratitude for being lucky and fortunate, of not having earned one's joy. And the experience seems complete in itself, without the need to look to the past or the future to give it importance.

Peak experiences are an example of the opposite of depressive experiences. Individuals who have learned to focus on depressive feelings often do not recognize feelings of happiness or satisfaction. By describing peak experiences, we hope to help you recognize them and appreciate their value.

Happiness and Satisfaction

Survey studies of subjective well-being have come up with an interesting finding. People seem to differentiate between "happiness" and "satisfaction." It seems that ratings of happiness are greatest during young adulthood and decrease (on the average) with age. Ratings of satisfaction are lowest during young adulthood and increase (on the average) with age. It may be that happiness is equated with emotionally charged enjoyment and satisfaction with more tranquil, peaceful (but probably equally deep) feelings of contentment.

Because this is the case, consider how this may affect your "peak experiences." During youth, they may be much more easily recognizable because the emotional arousal may be more intense. As you grow older, your peak experiences may be more mellow, and thus easier to overlook. It may be important, therefore, to learn to recognize and appreciate both types.

One thing should be clarified: The survey findings do *not* indicate that highly charged feelings of happiness disappear as people grow older, nor that young people never feel satisfied. What they do indicate is that "happiness" is more frequent in younger people and "satisfaction" is more frequent in older people.

A Final Note

As you consider putting into practice some of our suggestions, we would strongly advise you to consider the importance of *deciding.* Deciding on a course of action helps you feel more in control of your life. It is also a way to bear hard times when they come, because a decision made consciously has meaning behind it. Then, even if the decision doesn't lead to the best possible outcome, the meaning behind the decision gives it more intrinsic worth than a haphazard event. In addition, making a decision about your personal values and goals is a way to reduce the tendency to compare yourself to everyone else. No one else has exactly the same values and goals that you have. Thus, your efforts cannot be strictly compared to the efforts of other people.

Decide to follow or to put aside our suggestions and make this decision consciously. Decide even *not* to decide. We wish you success in your efforts and satisfaction with your continual progress.

REVIEW

- ☐ I have read about prevention and know what it is.
- ☐ I understand that planning is related to mental health.
- ☐ I have thought about my values and my goals, and I understand how they differ from one another.
- ☐ I realize how we strengthen or weaken our values by what we choose to come in contact with.
- ☐ I have written out the following:
    - ☐ My individual goals.
    - ☐ My interpersonal goals.
    - ☐ My philosophy of life.
- ☐ I have read about "peak experiences," and I think I could recognize a "peak experience" if I had one.
- ☐ I understand the difference between happiness and satisfaction.
- ☐ I have decided to do the following:
    - ☐ To try the suggestions that are made in this book.
    - ☐ Not to follow the suggestions that are made in this book.
    - ☐ Not to decide.

Suggestions for Further Reading

Throughout this appendix, references of special interest to the nonprofessional reader are indicated with an asterisk.

DEPRESSION

Akiskal, H.S., and W.T. McKinney, "Depressive Disorders: Toward a Unified Hypothesis," *Science*, 182 (1973), 20-29.

Anthony, J.E. and T. Benedek, *Depression and Human Existence*. Boston: Little, Brown, 1975.

Beck, A.T., *Depression: Clinical, Experimental, and Theoretical Aspects*. New York: Harper and Row, 1967.

Becker, J., *Depression: Theory and Research*. New York: V.H. Winston & Sons, 1974.

Becker, J., *Affective Disorders*. Morristown, N.J.: General Learning Press, 1977.

Davidson, P.O. (Ed.), *The Behavioral Management of Anxiety, Depression, and Pain*. New York: Brunner/Mazel, 1976.

Fann, W.E., I. Karacan, A.D. Pokerny, and R.L. Williams, *Phenomenology and Treatment of Depression*. New York: Spectrum Publications, 1977.

Friedman, R.J. and M.M. Katz, *The Psychology of Depression: Contemporary Theory and Research*. Washington, D.C.: V.H. Winston & Sons, 1974.

Greenacre, P. (Ed.), *Affective Disorders—Psychoanalytic Contributions to Their Study*. New York: International Universities Press, 1953.

Grinker, R.R., J. Miller, M. Sabshin, R. Nunn, and J.C. Nunally, *The Phenomena of Depressions*. New York: Paul B. Hoeber, Inc., 1961.

Klerman, G.L., M.M. Weissman, B.J. Rounsaville, and E.S. Chevron, *Interpersonal Psychotherapy of Depression*. New York: Basic Books, 1984.

*Kline, N.S., *From Sad to Glad*. New York: Ballantine Books, 1975.

Lewinsohn, P.M., "Clinical and Theoretical Aspects of Depression," in K.S. Calhoon, H.E. Adams, and K.M. Mitchell, (Eds.), *Innovative Methods in Psychopathology*. New York: John Wiley & Sons, 1974, pp. 63–120.

Lewinsohn, P.M., "The Behavioral Study and Treatment of Depression." In M. Hersen, R.M. Eisler, and P.M. Miller, (Eds.), *Progress in Behavior Modification*. Academic Press, 1975, pp. 19-64.

Lewinsohn, P.M. and M.A. Youngren, "The Symptoms of Depression," *Comprehensive Therapy*, 2 (1976), 62–69.
Mendels, J., *Concepts of Depression*. New York: Wiley & Sons, 1970.
Nevringer, C. (Ed.), *Psychological Assessment of Suicidal Risk*. Springfield, Ill.: Charles C. Thomas, 1974.
Paykel, E.S. (Ed.), *Handbook of Affective Disorders*. New York: Guilford, 1982.
Rush, A.J. (Ed.), *Short-term Psychotherapies for Depression*. New York: Guilford, 1982.
Seligman, M.E.P., *Helplessness*. New York: W.H. Freeman, 1975.
Silverman, C., *The Epidemiology of Depression*. Baltimore: The Johns Hopkins Press, 1968.
Weissman, M.M. and E.P. Paykel, *The Depressed Woman: A Study of Social Relationships*. Chicago: University of Chicago Press, 1974.
Whybrow, P.C., H.S. Akiskel, and W.T. McKinney, Jr., *Mood Disorders: Toward a New Psychobiology*. New York: Plenum, 1984.
Williams, T., M. Katz, and J. Shields (Eds), *Recent Advances in the Psychobiology of Depressive Illness*. Washington, D.C.: Government Printing Office, 1972.
Zeiss, A.M., P.M. Lewinsohn, and R.F. Muñoz, "Nonspecific Improvement Effects in Depression Using Interpersonal, Cognitive, and Pleasant Effects Focused Treatments," *Journal of Consulting and Clinical Psychology*, 47 (1979), 427-439.

SOCIAL LEARNING THEORY

Bandura, A., *Principles of Behavior Modification*. New York: Holt, Rinehart, & Winston, 1969.
*Bandura, A., "A Social Learning Interpretation of Psychological Dysfunctions," in P. London and D. Rosenhan (Eds.), *Foundations of Abnormal Psychology*. New York: Holt, Rinehart, & Winston, 1968, pp. 293-344.
Bandura, A., *Social Learning Theory*. Englewood Cliffs, N.J.: Prentice-Hall, 1977.
Kanfer, F.H. and A.P. Goldstein (Eds.), *Helping People Change*. New York: Pergamon Press, 1975.
Krumboltz, J. and C. Thorensen, *Counseling Methods*. New York: Holt, Rinehart, & Winston, 1976.

BEHAVIORAL SELF-MANAGEMENT

Fuchs, C.Z. and L.P. Rehm, "A Self-Control Behavior Therapy Program for Depression," *Journal of Consulting and Clinical Psychology*, 45 (1977), 206–215.
Goldfried, M.R. and M. Merbaum, (Eds.), *Behavior Change through Self-Control*. New York: Holt, Rinehart & Winston, 1973.
Kanfer, F.H. and A.P. Goldstein (Eds.), *Helping People Change*. New York: Pergamon Press, 1975.
*Mahoney, M.J. and C.E. Thoresen, *Self-Control: Power to the Person*. Monterey, California: Brooks/Cole, 1974.
Thoresen, C.E. and M.J. Mahoney, *Behavioral Self Control*. New York: Holt, Rinehart & Winston, 1974.
*Watson, D.L. and R.G. Tharp, *Self-Directed Behavior: Self-Modification for Personal Adjustment*. (4th edition). Monterey, California: Brooks/Cole, 1985.

RELAXATION

*Rosen, G.M., *The Relaxation Response*. Englewood Cliffs, N.J.: Prentice-Hall, 1977.
*Benson, H., *The Relaxation Response*. New York: William Morrow, 1975.

SOCIAL INTERACTION

General References
*Gambrill, E. and C.A. Richey, *It's Up to You: The Development of Assertive Social Skills*. Millbrae, Calif.: Les Femmes, 1976.

Glaser, S.R. *Toward Communication Competency*. New York: Holt, Rinehart & Winston, 1968.

*Johnson, S.M., *First Person Singular: Living the Good Life Alone*. Philadelphia, Pa.: Lippincott, 1977.

Weissman, M.M. and E.S. Paykel, *The Depressed Woman: A Study of Social Relationships*. Chicago, Ill.: University of Chicago Press, 1974.

Youngren, M.A. and P.M. Lewinsohn, "The Functional Relationship between Depression and Problematic Interpersonal Behavior," *Journal of Abnormal Psychology*, 89 (1980), 333-341.

*Zimbardo, P.G., *Shyness: What It Is, What to Do About It*. Reading, Mass.: Addison-Wesley, 1977.

*Zunin, L. and N. Zunin, *Contact: The First Four Minutes*. New York: Ballantine, 1972.

Assertion
*Alberti, R.E. and M. Emmons, *Your Perfect Right* (2nd edition). San Luis Obispo, Calif.: Impact, 1974.

*Bower, S.A. and G.H. Bower, *Asserting Your Self: A Practical Guide for Positive Change*. Reading, Mass.: Addison-Wesley, 1976.

Cotter, S.B. and J.J. Gruerra, *Assertion Training*. Champaign, Ill.: Research Press, 1976.

*Fensterheim, H. and J. Baer, *Don't Say Yes When You Want to Say No*. New York: Dell, 1975.

Kazdin, A.E., "Effects of Covert Modeling and Model Reinforcement on Assertive Behavior," *Journal of Abnormal Psychology*, 83 (1974), 240-252.

Kazdin, A.E., "Covert Modeling, Imagery Assessment, and Assertive Behavior," *Journal of Consulting and Clinical Psychology*, 43 (1975), 716–724.

Phelps, S. and A. Austin, *The Assertive Woman*. San Luis Obispo, Calif.: Impact, 1975.

Rich, A.R. and H.E. Schroeder, "Research Issues in Assertiveness Training," *Psychological Bulletin*, 83 (1976), 1081–1096.

Sanchez, V.C., P.M. Lewinsohn, and D. Lorson, "Assertion Training: Effectiveness in the Treatment of Depression," *Journal of Clinical Psychology*, 36 (1980), 526–529.

Smith, M.J., *When I Say No, I Feel Guilty*. New York: Bantam Books, 1975.

Nonverbal Behavior
Ekman, P. and W.V. Friesen, "Nonverbal Behavior and Psychopathology." In R.J. Friedman and M.M. Katz (Eds.), *The Psychology of Depression: Contemporary Theory and Research*. New York: Wiley, 1974.

PLEASANT EVENTS

Lewinsohn, P.M. and D.J. MacPhillamy, "The Relationship between Age and Engagement in Pleasant Activities," *Journal of Gerontology*, 29 (1974), 290–294.

Lewinsohn, P.M. and J. Libet, "Pleasant Events, Activity Schedules and Depression," *Journal of Abnormal Psychology*, 79 (1972), 291–295.

Lewinsohn, P.M. and M. Graf, "Pleasant Activities and Depression," *Journal of Consulting and Clinical Psychology*, 41 (1973), 261–268.

Lewinsohn, P.M., "Activity Schedules in the Treatment of Depression," in C.E. Thoresen, and J. Krumboltz (Eds.), *Counseling Methods*. New York: Holt, Rinehart & Winston, 1976, pp. 74–83.

Lewinsohn, P.M., M.A. Youngren, and S.C. Grosscup, "Reinforcement and Depression," in R.A. Depue, (Ed.), *The Psychobiology of the Depressive Disorders: Implications for the Effects of Stress.* New York: N.Y. Academic Press, 1979.

Teri L. and P.M. Lewinsohn, "Modification of the Pleasant and Unpleasant Effects Schedules for Use with the Elderly," *Journal of Consulting and Clinical Psychology*, 50 (1982), 444–445.

MacPhillamy, D.J. and P.M. Lewinsohn, "The Pleasant Events Schedule: Studies in Reliability, Validity, and Scale Intercorrelation," *Journal of Clinical and Consulting Psychology*, 50 (1982), 363-380.

COGNITIVE APPROACHES

Beck, A.T., A.J. Rush, B.J. Shaw, and G. Emery, *Cognitive Theory of Depression.* New York: Guilford, 1979.

Burns, D.D., *Feeling Good: The New Mood Therapy.* New York: Morrow, 1980.

Ellis, A. and R.A. Harper, *A Guide to Rational Living.* Hollywood, Calif: Wilshire Book Co., 1973.

Kranzler, G., *You Can Change How You Feel.* Eugene, Oregon: University of Oregon Press, 1974.

Mahoney, M.J., "The Self-Management of Covert Behavior: A Case Study," *Behavior Therapy*, 2 (1971), 575-578.

Mahoney, M.J., *Cognition and Behavior Modification.* Cambridge, Mass.: Ballinger, 1974.

Meichenbaum, D., "Self-Instructional Methods," in F.H. Kafner and A.P. Goldstein (Eds.), Helping People Change. New York: Pergamon, 1975.

Meichenbaum, D., *Cognitive-Behavior Modification: An Integrative Approach.* New York: Plenum Press, 1977.

Meichenbaum, D. and R. Cameron, "The Clinical Potential of Modifying What Clients Say to Themselves," in M.J. Mahoney and C.E. Thoreson (Eds.), *Self-Control: Power to the Person.* Monterey, Calif.: Brooks/Cole, 1974.

Stampfl, T.G. and D.J. Levis, "Essentials of Implosive Therapy: A Learning-Theory-Based Psychodynamic Behavioral Therapy," *Journal of Abnormal Psychology*, 72 (1967), 469-503.

CHANGING YOUR PERSONALITY

Kelly, G.A., *The Psychology of Personal Constructs*, Vols. 1 & 2. New York: Norton, 1955.

COPING WITH DEPRESSION COURSE

Brown, R. and P.M. Lewinsohn, *Participant Workbook for the Coping with Depression Course.* Eugene, Oregon: Castalia Publishing Company, 1984.

Brown, R. and P.M. Lewinsohn, "A Psychoeducational Approach to the Treatment of Depression: Comparison of Group, Individual, and Minimal Contact Procedures," *Journal of Consulting and Clinical Psychology*, in press. Lewinsohn, P.M., D.O. Antonuccio, J.L. Steinmetz, and L. Teri, *The Coping with Depression Course.* Eugene, Oregon: Castalia Publishing Company, 1984.

Steinmetz, J.L., L.W. Thompson, J.N. Breckenridge, and D. Gallagher, "Behavioral Group Therapy with the Elderly: A Psychoeducational Approach." In D. Upper and S. Ross (Eds.) *Handbook of Behavioral Therapy.* New York: Plenum Press, in press.

PREVENTIVE APPROACHES

Campbell, A., "Subjective Measures of Well-Being," in G.W. Albee and J.M. Joffee (Eds.), *Primary Prevention of Psychopathology.* Volume I: *The Issues.* Hanover, N.H.: University Press of New England, 1977.

Caplan, G. and H. Grunebaum, "Perspectives on Primary Prevention: A Review," in H. Gottesfeld (Ed.), *The Critical Issues of Community Mental Health.* New York: Behavioral Publications, 1972.

Kessler, J. and G.W. Albee, "Primary Prevention," *Annual Review of Psychology,* 26 (1975), 557-591.

Maslow, A.H., "Peak Experiences as Acute Identity-Experiences," *American Journal of Psychoanalysis,* 21 (1961), 254-260.

Maslow, A.H., *Toward A Psychology of Being.* (2nd ed.). New York: Van Nostrand Reinhold, 1968.

Maslow, A.H., *Motivation and Personality* (2nd ed.). New York: Harper & Row. 1970.

Muñoz, R.F., *Depression Prevention Research* New York: Hemisphere, in press.

Muñoz, R.F., "The Primary Prevention of Psychological Problems," *Community Mental Health Review,* 1 (6) (1976), 1–15.

Muñoz, R.F. and J.G. Kelly, *The Prevention of Mental Disorders.* Homewood, Ill.: Richard D. Irwin, 1975.

Shure, M.B. and G. Spivack, "Means-Ends Thinking, Adjustment, and Social Class among Elementary-School-Aged Children," *Journal of Consulting and Clinical Psychology,* 38 (1972), 348-353.

OTHER

Alcohol Problems

*Miller, W.R. and R.F. Muñoz, *How to Control Your Drinking* (Revised edition). Albuquerque: University of New Mexico Press, 1982.

Memory Problems

*Hisbee, K.L., *Your Memory: How It Works and How to Improve It.* Englewood Cliffs, N.J.: Prentice-Hall, 1977.

*Lorrayne, H. and J. Lucas, *The Memory Book.* Briarcliff Manor, N.Y.: Stein & Day, 1974.

*Young, M.N. and W.B. Gibon, *How to Develop an Exceptional Memory.* Hollywood, Calif.: Wilshire Books, 1973.

Phobias

*Rosen, G., *Don't Be Afraid: A Program for Overcoming Fears and Phobias.* Englewood Cliffs, N.J.: Prentice-Hall, 1976.

Sex and Marital Problems

*Barbach, L.G., *For Yourself: The Fulfillment of Female Sexuality.* New York: Doubleday, 1975.

*Gottman, J., C. Notarius, J. Gonso, and H. Markman, *A Couple's Guide to Communication.* Champaign, Ill.: Research Press, 1976.

*Heiman, J., L. LoPiccolo, and J. LoPiccolo, *Becoming Orgasmic: A Sexual Growth Program.* Englewood Cliffs, N.J.: Prentice-Hall, 1976.

Sleeping Problems

*Coates, T.J. and C.E. Thoresen, *How to Sleep Better.* Englewood Cliffs, N.J.: Prentice-Hall, 1977.

Extra Forms

Cut along the dashed lines and have additional copies of all of these forms made for your future use.

BECK DEPRESSION INVENTORY*

Instructions: This is a questionnaire. On the questionnaire are groups of statements. Please read the entire group of statements in each category. Then pick out the one statement in the group which best describes the way you feel *today,* that is, *right now.* Circle the number beside the statement you have chosen. If several statements in the group seem to apply equally well, circle each one.

Be sure to read all the statements in the group before making your choice.

A. (SADNESS)
- 0   I do not feel sad
- 1   I feel blue or sad
- 2a I am blue or sad all the time and I can't snap out of it
- 2b I am so sad or unhappy that it is quite painful
- 3   I am so sad or unhappy that I can't stand it

B. (PESSIMISM)
- 0   I am not particularly pessimistic or discouraged about the future
- 1   I feel discouraged about the future
- 2a I feel I have nothing to look forward to
- 2b I feel that I won't ever get over my troubles
- 3   I feel that the future is hopeless and that things cannot improve

C. (SENSE OF FAILURE)
- 0   I do not feel like a failure
- 1   I feel I have failed more than the average person
- 2a I feel I have accomplished very little that is worthwhile or that means anything
- 2b As I look back on my life all I can see is a lot of failure
- 3   I feel I am a complete failure as a person (parent, spouse)

D. (DISSATISFACTION)
- 0   I am not particularly dissatisfied
- 1   I feel bored most of the time
- 2a I don't enjoy things the way I used to
- 2b I don't get satisfaction out of anything any more
- 3   I am dissatisfied with everything

E. (GUILT)
- 0   I don't feel particularly guilty
- 1   I feel bad or unworthy a good part of the time
- 2a I feel quite guilty
- 2b I feel bad or unworthy practically all the time now
- 3   I feel as though I am very bad or worthless

F. (EXPECTATION OF PUNISHMENT)
- 0   I don't feel I am being punished
- 1   I have a feeling that something bad may happen to me
- 2   I feel I am being punished or will be punished
- 3a I feel I deserve to be punished
- 3b I want to be punished

*The authors wish to thank Aaron T. Beck, M.D., for granting permission to reprint the Beck Depression Inventory.

G. (SELF-DISLIKE)
- 0   I don't feel disappointed in myself
- 1a   I am disappointed in myself
- 1b   I don't like myself
- 2   I am disgusted with myself
- 3   I hate myself

H. (SELF-ACCUSATIONS)
- 0   I don't feel I am worse than anybody else
- 1   I am critical of myself for my weaknesses or mistakes
- 2   I blame myself for my faults
- 3   I blame myself for everything that happens

I. (SUICIDAL IDEAS)
- 0   I don't have any thoughts of harming myself
- 1   I have thoughts of harming myself but I would not carry them out
- 2a   I feel I would be better off dead
- 2b   I feel my family would be better off if I were dead
- 3a   I have definite plans about committing suicide
- 3b   I would kill myself if I could

J. (CRYING)
- 0   I don't cry any more than usual
- 1   I cry more than I used to
- 2   I cry all the time now. I can't stop it
- 3   I used to be able to cry but now I can't cry at all even though I want to

K. (IRRITABILITY)
- 0   I am no more irritated now than I ever am
- 1   I get annoyed or irritated more easily than I used to
- 2   I feel irritated all the time
- 3   I don't get irritated at all at things that used to irritate me

L. (SOCIAL WITHDRAWAL)
- 0   I have not lost interest in other people
- 1   I am less interested in other people now than I used to be
- 2   I have lost most of my interest in other people and have little feeling for them
- 3   I have lost all my interest in other people and don't care about them at all

M. (INDECISIVENESS)
- 0   I make decisions about as well as ever
- 1   I try to put off making decisions
- 2   I have great difficulty in making decisions
- 3   I can't make any decisions at all anymore

N. (BODY IMAGE CHANGE)
- 0   I don't feel I look any worse than I used to
- 1   I am worried that I am looking old or unattractive
- 2   I feel that there are permanent changes in my appearance and they make me look unattractive
- 3   I feel that I am ugly or repulsive looking

O. (WORK RETARDATION)
- 0   I can work as well as before
- 1a   It takes extra effort to get started doing something
- 1b   I don't work as well as I used to
- 2   I have to push myself very hard to do anything
- 3   I can't do any work at all

P. (INSOMNIA)
- 0   I can sleep as well as usual
- 1   I wake up more tired in the morning than I used to
- 2   I wake up 2–3 hours earlier than usual and find it hard to get back to sleep
- 3   I wake up early every day and can't get more than 5 hours' sleep

Q. (FATIGABILITY)
- 0   I don't get any more tired than usual
- 1   I get tired more easily than I used to
- 2   I get tired from doing nothing
- 3   I get too tired to do anything

R. (ANOREXIA)
- 0   My appetite is not worse than usual
- 1   My appetite is not as good as it used to be
- 2   My appetite is much worse now
- 3   I have no appetite at all

S. (WEIGHT LOSS)
- 0   I haven't lost much weight, if any, lately
- 1   I have lost more than 5 pounds
- 2   I have lost more than 10 pounds
- 3   I have lost more than 15 pounds

T. (SOMATIC PREOCCUPATION)
- 0   I am no more concerned about my health than usual
- 1   I am concerned about aches and pains or upset stomach or constipation
- 2   I am so concerned with how I feel or what I feel that it's hard to think of much else
- 3   I am completely absorbed in what I feel

U. (LOSS OF LIBIDO)
- 0   I have not noticed any recent change in my interest in sex
- 1   I am less interested in sex than I used to be
- 2   I am much less interested in sex now
- 3   I have lost interest in sex completely

Daily Mood Rating Form

Please rate your mood for this day (how good or bad you felt) using the 9-point scale shown. If you felt really great (the best you have ever felt or can imagine yourself feeling), mark 9. If you felt really bad (the worst you have ever felt or can imagine yourself feeling), mark 1. If it was a "so-so" (or mixed) day, mark 5.

If you felt worse than "so-so," mark a number between 2 and 4. If you felt better than "so-so," mark a number between 6 and 9. Remember, a low number signifies that you felt bad and a high number means that you felt good.

```
            very                                    very
        depressed_____happy
                  1  2  3  4  5  6  7  8  9
```

Enter the date on which you begin your mood ratings in Column 2 and your mood score in Column 3.

Monitoring Day	Date	Mood Score	Monitoring Day	Date	Mood Score
1			16		
2			17		
3			18		
4			19		
5			20		
6			21		
7			22		
8			23		
9			24		
10			25		
11			26		
12			27		
13			28		
14			29		
15			30		

Daily Relaxation Monitoring Form

Date: _____ to _____

Relaxation Rating: 0 = Most relaxed you have ever been
10 = Most tense you have ever been

	Monday	Tuesday	Wednesday	Thursday	Friday	Saturday	Sunday	Average Score (add your scores and divide by 7)
Average Score for the Day								
Least Relaxed Time								
Score								
When								
Where								
Situation								
Most Relaxed Time								
Score								
When								
Where								
Situation								
Occurrence of Tension Symptoms H = Headache SA = Stomachache SP = Sleep problem								
Relaxation Practice								
When								
For how long								
Score before								
Score after								

Daily Relaxation Monitoring for Problem Situations

Relaxation Rating: 0 = Most relaxed you have ever been
                   10 = Most tense you have ever been

Dates: _____ to _____

Problem Situations	Monday	Tuesday	Wednesday	Thursday	Friday	Saturday	Sunday
1.							
2.							
3.							
4.							
5.							
6.							
7.							
8.							
9.							
10.							

Activity Schedule

Activity	Day																														
	1	2	3	4	5	6	7	8	9	10	11	12	13	14	15	16	17	18	19	20	21	22	23	24	25	26	27	28	29	30
1																														
2																														
3																														
4																														
5																														
6																														
7																														
8																														
9																														
10																														
11																														
12																														
13																														
14																														
15																														
16																														
17																														
18																														

Activity Schedule

Activity	Day

Activity	1	2	3	4	5	6	7	8	9	10	11	12	13	14	15	16	17	18	19	20	21	22	23	24	25	26	27	28	29	30
19																														
20																														
21																														
22																														
23																														
24																														
25																														
26																														
27																														
28																														
29																														
30																														
31																														
32																														
33																														
34																														
35																														
36																														

Activity Schedule

Activity	Day

Day columns: 1 2 3 4 5 6 7 8 9 10 11 12 13 14 15 16 17 18 19 20 21 22 23 24 25 26 27 28 29 30

Activity rows: 37 38 39 40 41 42 43 44 45 46 47 48 49 50 51 52 53 54

Activity Schedule

Activity	Day 1	2	3	4	5	6	7	8	9	10	11	12	13	14	15	16	17	18	19	20	21	22	23	24	25	26	27	28	29	30
55																														
56																														
57																														
58																														
59																														
60																														
61																														
62																														
63																														
64																														
65																														
66																														
67																														
68																														
69																														
70																														
71																														
72																														

Activity Schedule

Activity	Day																													
	1	2	3	4	5	6	7	8	9	10	11	12	13	14	15	16	17	18	19	20	21	22	23	24	25	26	27	28	29	30
73																														
74																														
75																														
76																														
77																														
78																														
79																														
80																														
81																														
82																														
83																														
84																														
85																														
86																														
87																														
88																														
89																														
90																														

Activity Schedule

Activity	Day																													
---	1	2	3	4	5	6	7	8	9	10	11	12	13	14	15	16	17	18	19	20	21	22	23	24	25	26	27	28	29	30
91																														
92																														
93																														
94																														
95																														
96																														
97																														
98																														
99																														
100																														
Total for Day																														
Mood Score																														

**Chart for Recording Daily Pleasant
Activities and Mood Scores**

Number of Pleasant Activities

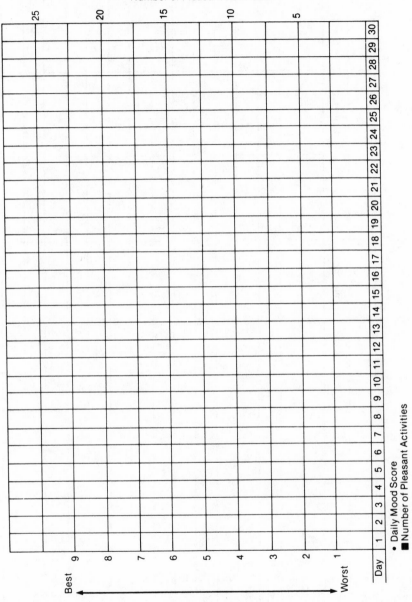

• Daily Mood Score
■ Number of Pleasant Activities

Weekly Plan

Date:															
Time	8:00	9:00	10:00	11:00	12:00	1:00	2:00	3:00	4:00	5:00	6:00	7:00	8:00	9:00	10:00
Monday															
Tuesday															
Wednesday															
Thursday															
Friday															
Saturday															
Sunday															

Self-Monitoring of Assertion Form

Situation	Comfort	Skill in Asserting Myself
1.		
2.		
3.		
4.		
5.		
6.		
7.		
8.		
9.		
10.		

Social Activities to Increase

Month: _____

Item Date:							
1.							
2.							
3.							
4.							
5.							
6.							
7.							
8.							
9.							
10.							
11.							
12.							
13.							
14.							
15.							
16.							
17.							
18.							
19.							
20.							
Daily Totals:							

Goal for Increasing: _____ per _____ .

Average Increase Achieved: _____ per _____ .

Interferences: Activities to Decrease

Item Date:							
Month: _____							
1.							
2.							
3.							
4.							
5.							
6.							
7.							
8.							
9.							
10.							
11.							
12.							
13.							
14.							
15.							
16.							
17.							
18.							
19.							
20.							
Daily Totals:							

Goal for Decreasing: _____ per _____ .

Average Decrease Achieved: _____ per _____ .

230

Daily Monitoring Form

Daily Monitoring Form[a]

Date _____

A. Activating Event

(Briefly describe the situation or event that seemed to lead to your emotional upset at C.)

B. Beliefs or Self-Talk

(List each of the things that you said to yourself about A.)

1.

2.

3.

4.

5.

(Now go back and place a checkmark beside each statement that is non-constructive or "irrational.")

C. Emotional Consequences

(Describe and rate how you felt when A happened.)

I felt: _____

_____

Rating (0 = mildly upset; 5 = extremely upset): _____

D. Dispute of Self-Talk

(For each checked statement in Section B describe what you would ask or say to dispute your non-constructive self-talk.)

[a]Note: You should first complete Section C. Then go back and complete Section A and Section B. After the first week of self-monitoring, also complete Section D.

Role Sketch of _____

1. My highest priorities (life goals, major commitments, etc.)

2. Personal style

3. Relationships

4. Summary: I can be happy and successful because

5. In clearly specified ways, how is this person I hope to be different from my present self description?

INDEX

ABOUT THE AUTHORS

PETER M. LEWINSOHN received his Ph.D. in Psychology from the Johns Hopkins University in 1955. He has been on the faculties of the Temple University Medical School, Indiana University Medical School, and Southern Illinois University and for four years served as Chief Psychologist at the Larue D. Carter Memorial Hospital in Indianapolis. Dr. Lewinsohn currently is Professor of Psychology and Director of the Neuropsychology Laboratory at the University of Oregon, positions he has held since 1965. For five years he also served as the Director of the Training in Clinical Psychology. Dr. Lewinsohn is the author of many scientific articles on depression and has co-authored books on geropsychology as well as depression. He is a diplomate in Clinical Psychology, American Board of Examiners in Professional Psychology, and in 1978 was the recipient of the Professional Award of the Mental Health Association of Oregon.

RICARDO F. MUÑOZ received his Ph.D in Psychology from the University of Oregon in 1977. He is an Associate Professor of Psychology at the University of California, San Francisco. Dr. Munoz has co-authored books on self-control of drinking and in the area of community psychology as well as depression. His research focuses on the prevention of depression, with particular emphasis on low-income, minority, non-English-speaking outpatients. Dr. Muñoz presently directs the Depression Prevention Research Project and the cognitive behavioral treatment team of the Depression Clinic at San Francisco General Hospital.

MARY ANN YOUNGREN is also a graduate of the Clinical Psychology program at the University of Oregon, receiving her Ph.D in 1978. She is currently an Associate Professor of Psychology at Willamette University in Salem, Oregon. She teaches courses in abnormal psychology, theories of personality, psychological tests and measurements, and behavior modification, and serves as the co-director of the Psychology Internship Program. Dr. Youngren serves as consultant for an NIMH project involving the cross-cultural application of the psychoeducation model in *Control Your Depression* to selected communities of Native Americans in the Pacific Northwest.

ANTONETTE M. ZEISS received her Ph.D. in Psychology from the University of Oregon in 1977. She is currently the Director of the Interdisciplinary Team Training in Geriatrics Program at Palo Alto Veterans Administration Center in Palo Alto, California. Dr. Zeiss is also a Clinical Lecturer in the School of Medicine at Stanford University. Her research and clinical interests include treatment of depression in older adults, exploration of basic self-regulatory processes associated with depression, and evaluation of inter-disciplinary team treatment of health problems of the elderly.